SOFRAMIZ

Vibrant Middle Eastern Recipes
from Sofra Bakery & Cafe

ANA SORTUN AND MAURA KILPATRICK

PHOTOGRAPHY BY KRISTIN TEIG

TEN SPEED PRESS
Berkeley

SOFRAMIZ

INTRODUCTION

Beginning at 8 am, people from all walks of life pass through our door to gather, eat, and restore.

Morning regulars grab a coffee and a feta pogaca, a flaky biscuit made with shredded carrots and dill, for the road. Turkish breakfast orders are called out for pickup over the sounds of milk steaming and mixers kneading. Dozens of morning buns disappear from the pastry-lined shelves, and the sweet, warm smells of spices, butter, and herbs fill the air. The meze bar starts brimming with an assortment of vegetable, bean, and grain salads that will later be arranged on plates and platters. By 10 am, chefs are cooking flatbreads on a large plancha griddle for manoushe, a thin stuffed flatbread, and shawarma, a skinny burrito-like sandwich with roasted chicken or lamb. The pace starts to pick up before the line forms for lunch. Falafel are shaped, pickles are cut, lettuce and herbs are chopped, moussakas and lamb pies are assembled with thin slices of roasted eggplant and béchamel sauce, until everything is put in place to serve lunch. The morning practice of mixing, kneading, rolling, shaping, baking, and glazing ends by midday, and the chefs transition the routines to chopping, slicing, sautéing, roasting, and braising.

Suppliers pull up all day and unload ingredients, exchanging smiles with staff as they unload. Murat and Nuran Chavushian, the twins from Sevan Bakery, arrive with Turkish red pepper paste, bulgur wheat, labne, and haloumi cheese. The Greek yogurt arrives in five-gallon tubs, while lemons, rose harissa, and local peaches are delivered by a favorite driver from Specialty Foods Boston. Chafic Malouf from Olive Harvest pulls in fifteen cases of his own Lebanese olive oil with kisses for each cheek, and at the same time, the milkman arrives. By early afternoon, Siena Farms

(owned and operated by Ana's husband, Chris Kurth) drops off the morning's vegetable harvest and more than one hundred CSA boxes for customers to pick up throughout the day.

By late afternoon it quiets down for lingerers sipping tea on the banquette as the early-evening crowd arrives to buy pumpkin jam, farm eggs, and hot pepper labne from the refrigerated case. Before the doors are closed, shelves are stocked with spice blends, small-batch tahinis, pomegranate molasses, olive oils, jams, pickles, packaged cookies, and nuts. The open, lime green–tiled kitchen rests for a few hours before the early-morning bakers arrive to begin the new day's baking.

Sofra grew quickly into a life of its own, but not without a few hiccups. During our early months, guests would clog up the line staring at the menu, unfamiliar with much of Middle Eastern cuisine. So we hired a hospitality manager to answer questions, guide them patiently through their decisions, and expedite the line to the register. Today there are many of us that make up the team at Sofra—bakers, chefs, cooks, prep cooks, dishwashers, retail managers, catering managers, a staff manager, packers, and many talented baristas. With so many moving parts in a small space, we developed a consistent rhythm and routine in order for things to fall into place. Every day, we practice what we know and love the most: baking, cooking, brewing, and serving vibrant Middle Eastern food with hospitality matching what we have encountered on our trips to Turkey and beyond.

We opened Sofra Bakery and Cafe in 2008 after one such trip, where we experienced the rich yet light style of eating many meze (mainly vegetable preparations) as a meal. The variety was overwhelming, but nothing ever felt too heavy. We sampled thin stuffed flatbreads called gozleme; feta and yogurt with jams for breakfast; airy baklavas; a thick cream called kaymak; a hot, syrup-soaked cheese pastry called kunefe; savory biscuits perfumed with nigella seeds; and perfected sandwiches called durum. We also discovered the word *sofra*. *Sofra* encompasses everything you prepare for the table: food, place settings, glassware, décor, linens. Every sofra is unique—we couldn't even find two people who defined it the same way! If you come to each of our homes on a Sunday night, our sofras will be different but united in their

warmth of spirit. Sofra, or *soframiz* ("our sofra"), is a feeling as much as it is a place. It's a gesture of hospitality, inviting and evolving. It can be influenced by the weather, the mood, the guests, and the occasion. No two sofras are the same, but behind every sofra is a host hoping to give guests a memorable meal.

We began working together in 1996 at 8 Holyoke, a restaurant in Cambridge, Massachusetts, owned by Tunisian chef Moncef Meddeb. Moncef introduced us to North African flavors and ingredients like brik pastry, complex spice blends such as ras el hannout, and piquant condiments like harissa, and inspired us to blend them into a fresh, new, broader style of Mediterranean cooking.

In 2001, Ana opened Oleana Restaurant in Cambridge, whose cuisine centers on Middle Eastern and Mediterranean food with a strong lean towards Turkish, and she asked Maura, who had displayed remarkable creative talents in the restaurant's pastry kitchen, to head up the Oleana pastry team. Maura continues to develop the sweets and pastry at Oleana while Ana creates the savory dishes.

After working together for eighteen years and traveling to France, Turkey, and Lebanon, we have become united in our passions and approach. We believe in learning the rules before we break them, so we study technique, ingredients, and recipes constantly. When we make hummus or baklava, our approach is to see, taste, and read as many hummus or baklava recipes as possible and then reinterpret what we've learned. As a result, dishes like Warm Buttered Hummus, Spicy Lamb, and Pine Nuts (page 84) and

Chocolate Hazelnut Baklava (page 173) are invented because we find an affinity between cultures—we don't just do it to be creative but to push our own understanding of what a dish can be. Our recipes may not be traditional, but they follow the spirit of the original dish. Because we love and respect the regional food traditions of the Eastern Mediterranean, Sofra is about reinterpreting those traditions to make them accessible and inspiring for our guests here in Cambridge.

Sofra dishes have their own stories, and our dream is to see these dishes evolve into traditions for others. We offer them as building blocks so you can understand where the dishes come from and where they might go. When making fattoush, a traditional Lebanese bread salad made with sumac, we adapt to the season and add fresh ingredients like tart green apple or radish to brighten the flavors, textures, and colors and to slightly change the predictable. Likewise, orange flower water is used in a simple sugar glaze to bring rich, floral, and citrus flavors to a buttery breakfast bun, and tahini is added to a rich hot chocolate to give it an extra layer of flavor.

Our recipes are meant to be mixed and matched—one flatbread and one meze might make a nice lunch, but a more elaborate meal of twelve or more meze might go into the wee hours of the morning. Although we have our favorite pairings, our wish is for you to discover which of our combinations suit the season, your mood, the occasion, your sofra. These recipes have been collected and practiced for many years, both in the restaurant and in our own homes. We invite you to mix and match to make your own tradition of sofra with friends and family.

BREAKFAST

Breakfast in Turkey or Lebanon is a revelation to travelers because of the sheer variety of dishes that's displayed in small bowls and plates on the table. One of the best spreads in all of Istanbul is the breakfast at Van Kahvalti Evi in the Cihangir neighborhood, where the olives, tahini, stuffed flatbreads, egg dishes, vegetables, and cheeses cover the entire table.

Once you have a taste for that variety, it's hard to settle for just coffee and cereal. For some of us, breakfast starts with the basics like granola, hot cereal, or eggs. But you can easily transform even these staples into extraordinary fare when you bake your eggs in a spiced tomato sauce; add rye berries, chickpeas, and rose water to your hot cereal; or roast your granola with olive oil and Moroccan Spiced Almonds.

Breakfast is a serious meal at Sofra, with items on the menu such as simit (a cross between a bagel and a pretzel), raspberry–rose petal turnovers, sujuk (spicy sausage) fried rice, Greek yogurt parfait, tahini brioche, and our most popular Turkish breakfast platter. The signature morning bun was one of Maura's early creations. Sofra had just opened and Maura gave Ana a trial batch to take on the run. It rested on the passenger seat and, while driving, Ana took a small bite and immediately had to pull over, nearly weeping from pure joy. This sweet, fragrant roll glazed with orange blossom icing surpasses in flavor all other cinnamon rolls, with the citrus notes bringing the sweetness into sharp relief.

We realize that most people don't have much time to prepare breakfast. Some of these recipes may require you to start the work the night before or may be designated for weekends or days off. But we want to change the way you feel about breakfast, and convince you that it's more than a meal on the go. These recipes have become a part of our daily lives, and with good reason.

Shakshuka means "all mixed up" in Hebrew and is one of the most popular breakfast dishes in Israel and at Sofra. Many countries in the Middle East and Eastern Mediterranean claim a version of their own, like Tunisian chakchouka, made with peppers and harissa, and a Moroccan version made with lamb sausage and harissa. The eggs are poached directly in the spicy tomato sauce, so it's important that the sauce is well seasoned and warmed before you add the eggs. ◆ **ANA**

SERVES 6

SHAKSHUKA (BAKED EGGS WITH SPICY TOMATO SAUCE)

Spicy Tomato Sauce

2 tablespoons extra-virgin olive oil

4 teaspoons finely chopped garlic

1 (28-ounce) can diced tomatoes, including the liquid

1 teaspoon Maras pepper (see page 236)

1½ teaspoons hawayej (see page 10), or 1 teaspoon curry powder

1½ teaspoons freshly squeezed lemon juice

Kosher salt and freshly ground black pepper

6 eggs

Kosher salt

6 (6-inch) store-bought pita breads or 3 Sofra Pita Breads (page 69), split in half widthwise

½ cup zhoug (see page 217 and note below)

ZHOUG Shakshuka, no matter where it originates, should be spicy, so the zhoug (a spicy Yemenite herb sauce) is essential, adding both heat and brightness from the fresh herbs.

Preheat the oven to 350°F.

To make the spicy tomato sauce, in a large saucepan over low heat, combine the olive oil, garlic, tomatoes, Maras pepper, and hawayej. Simmer until the tomatoes are soft and melted, about 15 minutes. It is important to cook the sauce slowly so the tomatoes are soft enough to puree but don't reduce too much. Set the sauce aside to cool slightly.

Using an immersion blender and starting at low speed, puree the sauce, gradually increasing the speed as the mixture becomes smoother and resembles a silky tomato soup. Stir in the lemon juice and season with salt and pepper to taste. Cover and refrigerate up for up to 1 week or use immediately.

When you are ready to make the shakshuka, gently reheat the sauce and pour it into a 9 by 13-inch glass baking dish or six soufflé ramekins or small cazuelas (4 to 5 inches in diameter and at least 1 inch high).

To make in a 9 by 13-inch dish, first crack each egg into a small bowl or ramekin to ensure that the yolks stay intact. Using the back of a spoon, make a divot for each egg and slide it into the sauce, one at a time, so that it doesn't float on top; leave a little space between each egg.

To make in individual baking dishes, set the ramekins onto a baking sheet. Ladle about ½ cup sauce into each dish and, using the back of a spoon, make a divot for the egg. To ensure that the yolks stay intact, first crack each egg into a small bowl or ramekin, then slide it into the sauce.

Lightly season the eggs with salt and transfer to the oven. Bake until the egg whites are just barely set and the yolks are very loose, about 20 minutes.

❯ ❯ ❯

SHAKSHUKA (BAKED EGGS WITH SPICY TOMATO SAUCE)

Remove the shakshuka from the oven. Scoop one egg on top of each pita bread and carefully spoon a generous amount of tomato sauce from the pan over the top of the egg. Place 1 teaspoon of zhoug on top of each serving and pass around additional zhoug at the table. If serving the shakshuka individually, top each shakshuka with 2 teaspoons of zhoug and serve them with a spoon and the bread on the side so that you can use the bread or spoon to scoop up the sauce. Serve immediately with additional zhoug.

HAWAYEJ Our recipe calls for hawayej, or hawaij (pronounced ha-why-ge), a traditional Yemenite spice blend. Usually a mixture of cumin, caraway, turmeric, peppercorns, cardamom, and cloves, hawayej may be difficult to find; curry powder can be substituted. My favorite is blended by our friend and master spice blender Lior Lev Sercarz in New York. You can buy directly from him online at laboiteny.com or make your own by combining ¼ cup ground cumin, 2 tablespoons turmeric, 2 teaspoons ground cardamom, 1 tablespoon ground coriander, 3 tablespoons fresh ground pepper, and 1 teaspoon ground cinnamon. Mix well and store in an airtight container out of direct sunlight for up to 3 months.

This is the best and easiest pumpkin bread and not just because it's my grandmother's recipe. We use Long Island cheese pumpkins from Siena Farms for the puree. The cheese pumpkin is dense and contains more water than other varieties, so it is perfect for turning into a puree to be used in baking. If it's unavailable, smaller sugar pumpkins will work as well. Making your own pumpkin puree requires some work but it really makes a huge difference in the moistness, and the flavor, of course. If you must, use one can of pumpkin, not pumpkin pie filling. If you are using canned pumpkin, decrease the salt to 1 tablespoon. ◆ **MAURA**

MAKES 3 LOAVES

NANA'S PUMPKIN BREAD

3 cups pumpkin puree from
1 (3- to 4-pound) pie pumpkin,
or 1 (29-ounce) can pumpkin

1 cup water

1½ cups canola oil

6 cups sugar

6 eggs

5¼ cups all-purpose flour

1½ tablespoons salt

1 tablespoon baking soda

1½ tablespoons ground
cinnamon

1 tablespoon ground nutmeg

1 teaspoon ground allspice

To make the pumpkin puree, preheat oven to 400°F. Cut the pumpkin into 4- to 5-inch pieces. Using a metal spoon, remove the seeds and fibers from the centers. Place the pumpkin pieces with the skin side up on a baking sheet and bake for 40 minutes or until the flesh is tender enough to be pierced very easily with a knife. Test around the flesh in several places for even doneness. Remove from the oven and cool directly on the pan.

Spoon out the flesh, including any liquid, into a food processor. Process until very smooth. You will need 3 cups of fresh pumpkin. Extra pumpkin can be frozen or used for our Pumpkin Jam (page 224).

Preheat the oven to 350°F. Butter three 9-inch loaf pans.

Combine the water, canola oil, sugar, eggs, flour, salt, baking soda, cinnamon, nutmeg, and allspice in a stand mixer fitted with a paddle attachment. Add the pumpkin last. Mix on medium speed until the batter is completely smooth, with absolutely no lumps. Divide evenly among the loaf pans.

Bake until a knife inserted in the center of a loaf comes out clean, 1 hour to 1¼ hours. Set aside to cool in pans. Loaves can be frozen for up to 1 month.

Cassie Piuma, my partner and chef extraordinaire at Sarma restaurant (a sibling to Sofra and Oleana) in Somerville, Massachusetts, got us hooked on the eggs featured here, which are soft-boiled, breaded in kataifi pastry (similar to shredded phyllo), and then deep-fried. We add them to our version of the famous Turkish breakfast spread, which includes sliced cucumber, olives, thick yogurt, jams, and cheeses. ◆ **ANA**

SERVES 4

TURKISH-STYLE BREAKFAST

7 eggs, 4 left whole, 3 lightly beaten

6 tablespoons all-purpose flour

1 tablespoon whole milk

Kosher salt

½ cup panko-style bread crumbs

Half of a 16-ounce package kataifi pastry (see page 236)

4 ounces feta cheese, preferably barrel-aged Greek feta, cut into 1-inch cubes

1 cup plain whole-milk Greek yogurt

½ cup Rose Petal Jam (page 226), Pumpkin Jam (page 224), or your favorite jam

2 vine-ripened or heirloom tomatoes, peeled (see page 17) and sliced or cut into wedges

3 tablespoons extra-virgin olive oil

1 Persian or ½ English cucumber, very thinly sliced

½ cup Moroccan or Spanish cured black olives, pitted

4 cups canola oil, for frying

Bring a saucepan of water to a boil over high heat. Using a slotted spoon, gently slide the 4 whole eggs into the boiling water and cook for exactly 6 minutes.

Carefully drain the water from the pan and place the pot of eggs in the sink. Run cold water in a slow, light stream over the eggs until they are completely cool, 3 to 5 minutes, or drop them into an ice bath and let them sit for 3 to 5 minutes. When they are cold, peel the eggs and set them aside.

Put the flour on a plate. Combine the 3 beaten eggs, milk, and a pinch of salt in a shallow bowl and mix well. Put the bread crumbs on a plate.

Loosen the strands of kataifi until you have long threads. Roll each boiled egg in the flour, then dip into the beaten egg mixture. Wrap the strands of kataifi tightly around each egg and set aside until you are ready to serve.

Put the feta cubes in the remaining flour and then dip into the beaten egg mixture. Dredge them in the bread crumbs and set aside until you are ready to serve.

Place ¼ cup yogurt on the side of each plate and top with 2 table-spoons jam. Place one-quarter of the tomatoes on each plate, season lightly with salt, and drizzle with olive oil.

Combine the cucumber and 2 tablespoons of the olive oil in a small mixing bowl, toss well, and season with salt. Divide equally among the plates near the tomato. Divide the olives equally among the plates, placing them near the cucumber and the tomato.

❯ ❯ ❯

> > > **TURKISH-STYLE BREAKFAST**

Place a large saucepan or wok on the stove (or use a tabletop deep-fryer), add the canola oil, and heat until it reaches 325°F to 350°F.

Drop the feta cubes into the hot oil. Using a long-handled slotted spoon, lightly stir so that the cubes don't stick to the bottom. Deep-fry until the feta cubes are golden brown and crisp, 60 to 90 seconds, and drain on paper towels. Repeat the same process with the eggs, allowing about the same amount of time.

Divide the fried feta and fried eggs among the plates and serve right away.

DEEP-FRYING If you don't have a thermometer, test the temperature of the oil by dropping a popcorn kernel into the oil. It will pop at approximately 325°F.

In 2011, Maura and I took a trip to Lebanon to explore its rich cuisine and find inspiration for our menus. Our host, Chafic Maalouf, and his mother, Saidi Jehe-Malouf, made an extraordinary breakfast on our first morning, including a very thin rolled omelet filled with foraged wild greens and labne, served at room temperature. Equally good warm or cold, this omelet is great wrapped in parchment paper and taken on the road. ◆ **ANA**

SERVES 4

ROLLED OMELET WITH ZA'ATAR AND LABNE

3 tablespoons za'atar
(see page 245 and note below)

3 tablespoons plus 1 teaspoon extra-virgin olive oil

½ cup labne or whole-milk Greek yogurt (page 233)

2 green onions, white part only, finely chopped

1 to 2 tablespoons chopped pickled hot peppers, or 1 teaspoon minced fresh jalapeño

½ teaspoon kosher salt, plus more to taste

6 eggs, beaten

4 teaspoons all-purpose flour

1 tablespoon water

4 cups escarole, spinach, or arugula cut into thin ribbons

2 tablespoons chopped fresh spearmint leaves

Squeeze of fresh lemon juice

Maras pepper (see page 236), for garnish

In a small bowl, mix the za'atar with 2 tablespoons of the olive oil. Set aside.

In another bowl, mix the labne, green onions, and pickled hot peppers. Season with salt to taste and stir until smooth. Set aside.

In a bowl, whisk the eggs, flour, ½ teaspoon salt, and water until smooth. Don't worry about a few lumps. Pour into a liquid measuring cup.

In an 8-inch nonstick pan or cast-iron skillet, heat 1 teaspoon of the olive oil over low to medium-low heat. Pour one-quarter of the egg mixture into the skillet and swirl the pan to form a thin omelet. Try not to brown the omelet, so adjust the heat accordingly. Cook until the omelet is just set, 2 to 3 minutes, and slide it out of the pan onto a plate. Repeat until you have four thin omelets. You can layer them on top of each other as they are cooked.

Lay the omelets out onto a cutting board, tray, or baking sheet and divide the labne mixture equally among them. Using the back of a spoon or an offset spatula, spread the mixture out until it's evenly distributed over the surface. Divide the za'atar mixture evenly over the tops of the omelets and, using the back of a spoon or an offset spatula, spread until it's evenly distributed over the labne.

In a small mixing bowl, combine the escarole, mint, lemon juice, and remaining 1 tablespoon of olive oil and season with salt to taste. Divide the greens evenly over the top of each omelet and roll tightly. Garnish with Maras pepper. Serve warm or at room temperature.

ZA'ATAR Za'atar is a wild herb that grows in the mountains along the Eastern Mediterranean and is similar to summer savory (but related to thyme). Za'atar is also a spice blend made with the herb blended with sesame seeds and sumac. Za'atar is delicious combined with an equal measure of extra-virgin olive oil and eaten by the spoonful or spooned over warm olives, cheese pizza, roasted chicken, or cheese.

This is a hearty breakfast that resembles Chinese fried rice. I love combining the rice with bulgur wheat to give it that delicious nutty wheat flavor from the whole grain. Sujuk is a Middle Eastern dried beef sausage made with spices like cumin, Maras pepper, fenugreek, allspice, and garlic. You can substitute lamb merguez (a Moroccan-style sausage) for a different but equally delicious alternative. ◆ **ANA**

SERVES 4

EGG FRIED RICE WITH SUJUK, GREEN PEPPER, AND TOMATO

Garlicky Labne

1 teaspoon finely chopped garlic

2 teaspoons freshly squeezed lemon juice

Kosher salt

¼ cup labne or plain whole-milk Greek yogurt (see page 233)

1 cup short- to medium-grain rice, such as Spanish Calasparra (paella) rice or Turkish Baldo rice

1 cup coarse-ground bulgur wheat (see page 231)

1 tablespoon extra-virgin olive oil

8 ounces sujuk (see page 242), thick casing removed and thinly sliced

3 plum tomatoes, grated (see Cook's Note)

1 teaspoon Hungarian sweet paprika

1½ cups chopped Cubanelle peppers (about 2 peppers)

½ cup thinly sliced green onions, mostly the white part

Kosher salt and freshly ground black pepper

4 eggs, lightly beaten

To make the garlicky labne, in a small bowl, combine the garlic, lemon juice, and a pinch of salt; set aside for 5 minutes. Stir in the labne and season to taste with salt. Set aside.

Bring 6 cups water to a boil in a saucepan. Stir in the rice and when it returns to a boil, turn the heat down to low and simmer, stirring occasionally, until it is tender, about 20 minutes. Drain well and rinse under cold water.

In another saucepan, bring 2 cups water to a boil and add the bulgur. Stir the bulgur and simmer until tender, about 10 minutes. Drain and set aside to cool.

In a sauté pan, heat 1½ teaspoons olive oil over medium-low heat. Add the sujuk and cook until the sausage is slightly crisp and brown and has rendered some of its fat, about 5 minutes. Using tongs or a slotted spoon, transfer to a paper towel, leaving the rendered fat in the pan. Add the tomatoes, paprika, and Cubanelle peppers to the pan and cook, stirring from time to time, without browning, until the vegetables are tender, about 5 minutes. Stir in the green onions and season with salt to taste.

Transfer the mixture to a mixing bowl along with the pan drippings. Add the rice and bulgur and stir until coated. Season with salt and pepper to taste.

Using the same sauté pan, add the remaining 1½ teaspoons of olive oil. When the pan is hot, add the eggs, swirling the pan to make a thick omelet. Once the omelet starts to set, stir, breaking it up into large pieces.

Add the egg and reserved sujuk to the rice mixture and stir well, breaking up the egg into smaller pieces.

Again, using the same pan, reheat the fried rice over medium-low heat until the rice is hot and starts to get crispy along the edges, 7 to 8 minutes.

Serve in large bowls with a dollop of the garlicky labne.

COOK'S NOTE For peeling tomatoes, blanch the cored tomatoes in a large pot of boiling water for about 30 seconds if they are thin-skinned heirlooms or beefsteaks or for 1 minute if they are thick-skinned plum tomatoes. Immediately transfer them to a bowl of ice water or run them under cold water. When the tomatoes are cool enough to handle, simply peel away the skin; it should almost slip right off.

For grating tomatoes, cut the tomatoes in half widthwise. Using your fingers, scrape as many seeds out of the cavities of the tomato as you can without being too fussy. Over a bowl, use the large holes of a box grater to grate the tomatoes (holding the cut side of the tomato to the grater) until you have nothing but skin left in your hand and the flesh of the tomato is in the bowl. This fresh pulp is a great base for salsa, gazpacho, and tomato sauce. When mixed with olive oil and something acidic like vinegar or verjus, it makes a delicious sauce or dressing for fish or salad.

In 2014, I visited the farm of my friend chef Musa Dagdeviren outside of Istanbul, where he had recently built five replicas of ancient or antique Turkish wood-burning ovens. We made lamb tail confit katmer, or flatbreads, in one of the ovens, which inspired me to create this recipe. This style of katmer resembles the Chinese scallion pancake, using yufka, a nonyeasted dough made with milk, egg, and vinegar, which keep the dough tender. The yufka is rolled out like a tortilla and filled with a spreadable lamb sausage flavored with cumin and dried spearmint. It's then shaped into a rope, spiraled like a serpentine, and rolled out before cooking. These are best served hot, cut into wedges with a dollop of pistachio yogurt for a very rich breakfast, brunch, or lunch. This yufka dough recipe is slightly different from the yufka found on page 95, which is used in making our gozleme (sandwich flatbreads) and is a little more breadlike. ◆ **ANA**

MAKES 12 KATMER; SERVES 6 TO 12

LAMB SAUSAGE KATMER WITH PISTACHIO YOGURT

Yufka Dough

3⅓ cups (1 pound) all-purpose flour, plus more if needed

2½ teaspoons kosher salt

¾ cup water

½ cup whole milk

1 egg, lightly beaten

¼ cup canola oil

2 tablespoons white wine vinegar

Pistachio Yogurt

1 teaspoon finely chopped garlic

1 tablespoon freshly squeezed lemon juice

1 teaspoon kosher salt

1 cup plain whole-milk Greek yogurt or labne (page 233)

¾ cup very finely chopped lightly toasted pistachios

2 tablespoons chopped fresh flat parsley leaves

Freshly ground black pepper

ingredients continue on next page

Lightly flour a work surface.

To make the yufka dough, sift the flour and salt into a mixing bowl. Make a well in the middle of the flour and add the water, milk, egg, oil, and vinegar. Using your hands, draw the flour in from all sides, working the mixture until it forms a sticky ball. Turn out onto the floured surface and knead until it's smooth and elastic, about 3 minutes. If the dough is still very sticky, add a little more flour until it stops sticking to your hands. Divide the dough in half and then divide each half into six equal pieces; you should have twelve 2-inch balls.

Cover the dough with parchment paper or a clean towel and refrigerate for at least 2 hours, or up to overnight.

To make the pistachio yogurt, in a small mixing bowl, combine the garlic, lemon juice, and ½ teaspoon of the salt and set aside for 5 minutes to soften the raw flavor of the garlic. Whisk in the yogurt until it's smooth, then stir in the pistachio and parsley. Season with salt and pepper to taste. Set aside. (You can also do this in a food processor fitted with a metal blade to achieve a smoother texture and a brighter color of green.)

To make the lamb filling, in a mixing bowl, combine the lamb, cumin, spearmint, oregano, Maras pepper, black pepper, red pepper paste, egg white, and green onion until everything is smooth and creamy. Set aside.

❯ ❯ ❯

LAMB SAUSAGE KATMER
WITH PISTACHIO YOGURT

Lamb Filling

1 pound ground lamb shoulder or fatty lamb, 80 to 85 percent lean

1 teaspoon ground cumin

1 teaspoon dried spearmint

1 teaspoon dried oregano

½ teaspoon Maras pepper (see page 236)

½ teaspoon freshly ground black pepper

2 teaspoons Turkish red pepper paste (see page 244)

1 egg white

2 tablespoons finely chopped green onions, mostly the white part

Olive oil, for brushing

Kosher salt, for sprinkling

Lightly flour a work surface. Lightly flour a baking sheet.

Place one of the dough balls on the prepared work surface and roll out until 6 to 7 inches in diameter. Divide the lamb mixture into twelve portions, each weighing approximately 1¼ ounces. Place one of the lamb portions on the dough ball, flattening it out and spreading it on the dough gently without breaking or tearing the dough.

Make a hole in the center of each yufka and roll the dough from the inside to the outside, moving around the circle (see photos, right) so that you have a perfectly even round ring when you are finished. Cut the ring in the middle and coil it up like a serpentine. Tuck the tail into the center and place on the prepared baking sheet. Repeat the process with the remaining dough. (You can freeze the katmer at this point.)

Roll out each serpentine to 5 inches in diameter and ¼ inch thick, adding flour if needed and being careful not to roll so hard that the filling pushes out of the dough. Some may start to show through the dough, which is okay.

Lightly oil each side of the katmer by brushing with a little olive oil. Place a large cast-iron skillet over low heat. When it is hot, place two katmer (if you can fit them) in the skillet and cook until golden and crisp, about 4 minutes per side. When they are done, you will be able to see some of the juices from the lamb start to bubble out of the dough. Sprinkle lightly with salt and stack them on top of each other. Cover with foil to keep warm. Cut into wedges and serve with a generous amount of the pistachio yogurt.

COOK'S NOTE Katmer can be filled, coiled, and then frozen on a baking sheet. They will take about 20 minutes to thaw and then you can roll them out to flatten them before cooking as instructed above. If you have leftovers, these cooked katmer reheat beautifully in a toaster oven or conventional oven or on a cast-iron griddle.

Kohlrabi, a relative of the cabbage in the brassica family, is juicy and crisp, like the stem of broccoli. It thrives in the New England climate and is a spring and fall star at my husband's vegetable farm, Siena Farms, in Sudbury, Massachusetts. This recipe is a staple in my home and my restaurants and is always a hit with our CSA members. ◆ **ANA**

MAKES 12 SMALL PANCAKES; SERVES 6

KOHLRABI PANCAKES WITH BACON AND HALOUMI CHEESE

4 cups peeled and grated kohlrabi (about 3 pounds)

1 teaspoon kosher salt

6 slices bacon

¼ cup finely chopped green onions, mostly the white part

¼ cup finely chopped fresh flat-leaf parsley leaves

¼ cup finely chopped fresh spearmint leaves

¼ cup finely chopped fresh dill leaves

6 to 8 ounces haloumi cheese, grated on the small holes of a box grater (see Cook's Note), plus additional for garnish

1 tablespoon plain whole-milk Greek yogurt or labne (see page 233)

1 egg

½ teaspoon freshly ground black pepper

½ cup all-purpose flour, plus more if needed

1 tablespoon baking powder

3 cups shredded spinach or Swiss chard leaves, stems discarded

3 to 4 tablespoons grapeseed oil or extra-virgin olive oil

Combine the kohlrabi and salt in a colander set over a plate or shallow bowl and set it aside until it loses its liquid, about 10 minutes.

Meanwhile, cook the bacon over medium-low heat until the fat is rendered and the bacon is crispy, about 3 minutes on each side. Drain on paper towels and coarsely chop.

Squeeze the kohlrabi dry by putting small amounts between your palms and squeezing until the liquid runs dry.

In a mixing bowl, combine the kohlrabi, green onions, parsley, mint, dill, 1 cup grated haloumi cheese, yogurt, egg, and black pepper and stir until combined. Sift in the flour and baking powder. Stir to combine and fold in the spinach. If the spinach is really wet, you may need to add a little more flour to keep the mixture together.

In a nonstick skillet, heat 1 tablespoon of the oil over medium-low heat. The pan should not be too hot or the haloumi will burn easily. Using a quarter-cup measure, drop some of the kohlrabi mixture into the pan. Flatten each pancake with the back of a spatula. Add one or two more pancakes, depending on the size of the pan. Be sure to have a little room between each pancake if you cook two or more at a time; if you crowd the pan, the pancakes will not brown.

Cook each pancake until evenly browned and really hot in the center, 3 to 4 minutes per side. They are fragile when you flip them over, so use a large spatula to turn them. Wipe the pan in between batches with a paper towel. Repeat until all the pancakes are cooked.

Cool the pancakes on a wire rack until you are ready to serve. Reheat the pancakes in the oven or on the stovetop and sprinkle with the chopped bacon and additional haloumi cheese.

COOK'S NOTE The microplane works wonderfully for powdering haloumi over something hot like these pancakes before serving (but I recommend using the box grater to get a whole cup's worth for the recipe). I also love the combination of all the fresh herbs in this pancake—the traditional Turkish blend is equal parts parsley, mint, and dill, which we call PMD in Sofra's kitchen. If you don't have fresh herbs on hand, use 2 teaspoons dried spearmint instead.

This pancake, or fritter, can be transformed by substituting daikon radish, sweet white turnips, parsnips, or zucchini for the kohlrabi or adding shredded Swiss chard in place of the spinach. You can make the batter a day ahead, cover, and refrigerate overnight. If the batter becomes too wet from additional water leaching out of the kohlrabi, mix it again and add another tablespoon or two of flour.

HALOUMI CHEESE Haloumi cheese is a sheep's milk cheese from Cyprus that is cooked and then brined. Because it is cooked, it can be sliced and put straight in a pan to caramelize without being breaded. It's best eaten very hot as it has a squeaky texture like cheese curds when it cools down. Haloumi is often seasoned with dried spearmint, which adds a sweet warmth to the cheese.

Pogaca is a roll commonly served for breakfast in Turkey. The dough here also makes a perfect, soft white dinner roll, but when rolled out, filled with feta cheese, and shaped into a beautiful rose, the rolls are a showstopper. Everyone loves butter rolls and will likely never have seen anything quite like these. If you take the time to form the roses, your guests will be so impressed. ◆ **MAURA**

MAKES 12 ROLLS

FLOWER POGACA ROLLS

1 cup whole milk, warmed to 105°F

1 tablespoon active dry yeast

2 teaspoons sugar

1 large egg

½ cup canola oil

3¼ cups all-purpose flour

2 teaspoons kosher salt

12 ounces crumbled feta cheese

¼ cup chopped fresh flat-leaf parsley leaves

Egg Wash

2 eggs

2 teaspoons whole milk

In the bowl of a stand mixer, whisk together by hand the warm milk, yeast, and sugar. Set aside until foamy, about 5 minutes.

Whisk in the egg and canola oil. Add the flour and salt. Using a dough hook, mix on low speed until the flour is incorporated. Increase the speed to medium-low and knead until smooth, about 8 minutes.

Lightly flour a work surface, turn out the dough, and knead into a smooth ball. Place the dough in a clean, lightly oiled bowl. Cover with plastic wrap and let rise at room temperature until doubled in size, 1 to 1½ hours.

Lightly flour a work surface and turn the dough out. Divide into 12 to 14 equal-size pieces (weighing approximately 2 ounces each) and roll each into a smooth ball. Cover with plastic wrap and let rest for 30 minutes.

Combine the feta and parsley in a small bowl.

Line a baking sheet with parchment paper. Lightly flour a work surface.

Roll each ball into a 5-inch circle. Cut four slits, each about 1½ inches long, starting from the edges and going toward the center at the north, south, east, and west ends of the balls (see photos, page 27). Place a generous tablespoon of the feta and parsley mixture in the center of the dough. Starting at the top, fold that quarter of the dough over the cheese. The dough will partially cover but not enclose the cheese. Fold about ¼ inch of the dough edge back to form an open petal. Fold the dough quarter at the bottom over the cheese and fold back the top to form an open petal. Fold the right side over the cheese, folding back to form a petal. When folding the final quarter over, tuck the edges underneath the rose, folding back that piece to form a petal. Place on the prepared baking sheet. Repeat with the remaining balls of dough, leaving two inches in between the rolls.

❯ ❯ ❯

▸ ▸ ▸ FLOWER POGACA ROLLS

Cover with plastic wrap and let rise at room temperature until almost doubled, 30 to 45 minutes.

Preheat the oven to 350°F.

Whisk together the eggs and milk to make an egg wash. Brush the rolls with the egg wash, then bake until golden brown, 25 to 30 minutes. Rolls can be served warm or at room temperature, and are best eaten the day they are made.

COOK'S NOTE The soft dough can also be rolled into individual soft rolls and stuffed with the feta and parsley for a more traditional pogaca. The dough also makes a beautiful soft roll without filling.

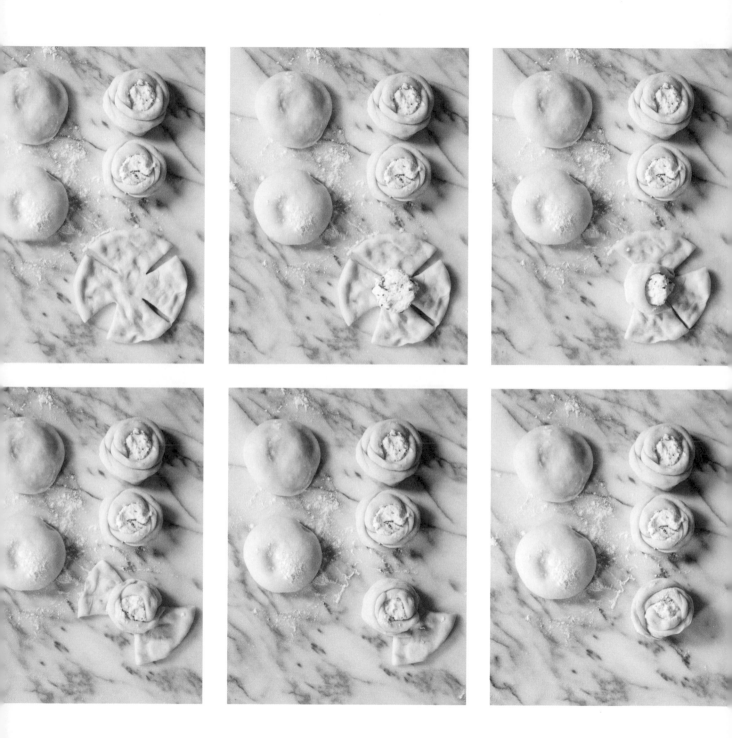

Pogaca is a tender, buttery roll. It can be a biscuit like this one, or yeasted, like in our flower version (page 25). Ana's friend Hamza Yildiz, who lives in Istanbul, introduced us to a golden pogaca made with grated carrot, dill, and cornmeal. Hamza helped research some recipes originating from the Black Sea region in Turkey, which influenced me to create this beautiful, crunchy, buttery pogaca. ◆ **MAURA**

MAKES 12 TO 14 ROLLS

FETA AND DILL POGACA

2⅓ cups all-purpose flour

1 cup coarse cornmeal

2 tablespoons sugar

3 tablespoons baking powder

2 teaspoons kosher salt

2 tablespoons chopped
fresh dill leaves

½ cup peeled, grated carrot
(about 1 large)

1 stick (4 ounces) chilled unsalted
butter, cut into ¼-inch cubes

2 eggs

1 cup plain whole-milk
Greek yogurt

6 ounces crumbled feta cheese

1 teaspoon whole milk

2 tablespoons nigella seeds

Preheat the oven to 350°F. Line a baking sheet with parchment paper. Lightly flour a work surface.

In the bowl of a stand mixer fitted with a paddle attachment, combine the flour, cornmeal, sugar, baking powder, salt, dill, carrot, and cubed butter. Mix on low speed until the mixture is crumbly and the butter is in pea-size pieces, about 3 minutes.

In a small bowl, mix 1 egg and the yogurt. Add to the stand mixer and mix on low until just combined. The dough will be wet. Add the feta but do not mix it in completely.

Transfer the dough to the work surface and, by hand, finish working in the feta until the dough is smooth. Flatten into a 5 by 10-inch rectangle and cut into 2½ by 2½-inch square biscuits. Place on the prepared baking sheet 2 inches apart. Whisk together the remaining egg and milk. Brush the tops of each pogaca with the egg mixture, then sprinkle the tops with nigella seeds.

Bake until very lightly browned, 20 to 25 minutes. Cool completely on the baking sheet. Serve at room temperature.

This subtle, savory, and nutty dough takes a lot of time, but it is worth every second. We start with a sponge, which helps the deep flavor of tahini come through. This recipe makes 2 pounds of dough, enough for two loaves of bread or, if shaped individually, 12 sandwich or dinner rolls. I have included a recipe for turning this beautiful dough into the base of a sweet cheese tart (page 33), for which you will need only one-quarter of a batch of dough. ◆ **MAURA**

MAKES 2 POUNDS DOUGH, ENOUGH FOR 2 LOAVES, 12 DINNER ROLLS, OR 4 TART SHELLS

TAHINI BRIOCHE DOUGH

Sponge

¼ cup whole milk, warmed to 100°F to 110°F

2¼ teaspoons active dry yeast

½ teaspoon sugar

2 eggs

1⅓ cups all-purpose flour

Dough

1⅓ cups all-purpose flour

¼ cup sugar

1 tablespoon salt

3 eggs plus 1 egg yolk

6 tablespoons tahini (see Cook's Note below and page 242)

1¾ sticks (7 ounces) unsalted butter, chilled and cut into ½-inch cubes

To prepare the sponge, combine the milk, yeast, and sugar in the bowl of a stand mixer. Whisk by hand to dissolve the yeast. Whisk in the eggs. Stir in 1 cup of the flour and sprinkle the remaining ⅓ cup over the top. Set aside to proof until there are cracks in the top layer and it is very soft to the touch, about 30 minutes.

To make the dough, add the flour, sugar, salt, eggs, egg yolk, and tahini to the bowl with the sponge. Using a dough hook, start mixing on low speed until the dough starts to come together. Increase to medium speed and mix until you can see the dough come together around the dough hook, 8 to 10 minutes. It is important that the dough is developed before you incorporate the butter.

Scrape the sides of the bowl. Mix again on high speed, and add half of the butter. Once the first half of the butter has been incorporated, add the second half. Continue mixing until the dough is silky smooth, 10 to 15 minutes. Increase the speed to medium-high and beat until the dough comes off the bowl, about 1 minute. You should be able to stretch a piece of dough to form a gluten window, meaning the gluten is fully developed, which is one of the most satisfying parts about making brioche.

Lightly flour a bowl or plastic storage container. Scrape the dough into the container and press it out into a flat rectangle. Fold the two sides in to meet in the middle, then flip the dough over and press it out into a flat rectangle. Cover and refrigerate for at least 6 hours, or up to overnight. After refrigerating, the dough will be ready to form into bread or rolls or a sweet or savory tart. At this point, you can shape it into your preferred shapes and freeze it. The dough will keep in the freezer for up to 5 days.

COOK'S NOTE Tahini sometimes has a separate layer of oil, so be sure to stir it well before measuring.

This bread freezes beautifully when completed, and you will be happy to have an extra loaf to pull from your freezer. ◆ **MAURA**

MAKES 2 LOAVES OR 12 ROLLS

TAHINI BRIOCHE LOAVES OR DINNER ROLLS

2 pounds Tahini Brioche Dough (page 29), cold

2 eggs

2 teaspoons whole milk

2 to 3 tablespoons sesame seeds, toasted (see page 241)

To make loaves, lightly flour a work surface. Butter two 9-inch loaf pans. Divide the dough in half. On the work surface, roll one half of the dough into a 12 by 6-inch rectangle. Divide into three strips. Start at the top and braid the strands together. Fit into one of the prepared loaf pans. Repeat with the second piece of dough.

Cover loaves with plastic wrap. Let sit at room temperature until doubled in size, 2 to 2½ hours, with the dough almost reaching the top of the pan. To test to see if the loaf is properly proofed, press down with your finger. It should feel like a soft pillow and spring back almost all the way, still leaving an indentation.

Preheat the oven to 350°F.

Whisk the eggs with the milk to make an egg wash, then brush loaves with the egg wash and sprinkle the tops with sesame seeds. Bake until golden brown, 40 to 45 minutes. Let cool in pans on a wire rack.

To make rolls, lightly flour a work surface. Butter a 9-inch springform pan; set aside. Divide the dough into 12 pieces. The rolls should fit into a springform pan; if you have additional rolls, you can bake them on a baking sheet. Using a cupped hand, gently roll each piece using small circular motions, applying steady pressure until a tight ball forms. Repeat with the remaining pieces to form rolls. Arrange the rolls in the prepared pan in a single layer, with 8 rolls around the rim and 4 rolls in the center. The springform pan gives you a beautiful presentation; simply by unsnapping the pan, you have a perfect circle.

Cover loosely with plastic wrap. Let rise at room temperature until almost doubled in size, 1½ to 2 hours.

> > >

▸ ▸ ▸ TAHINI BRIOCHE LOAVES OR DINNER ROLLS

To test to see if they are properly proofed, press down on a roll with your finger. It should feel like a soft pillow and spring back almost all the way, still leaving an indentation.

Preheat the oven to 350°F.

To make the egg wash, whisk together the eggs and milk. Brush the rolls with the egg wash and sprinkle sesame seeds over the tops.

Bake until golden brown, 15 to 20 minutes. Snap off the outside of the springform pan and let cool on the pan bottom on a wire rack. Other rolls can cool on the baking sheet.

To make this tart, the dough is pressed out in a cake pan, then topped with cheese and soft, cooked dates. Pastry chefs are always looking for ways of creating texture; one of our favorite ways is with a crumble or streusel. Topping this with a halvah crumb is perfect, but another option is drizzling the Orange Blossom Glaze (see page 45) over the top after the tart has cooled. The tahini brioche can easily be used as a base for a savory tart also. Follow the same instruction for filling the springform pan and create a sweet or savory tart of your own. It is perfect for Thanksgiving with roasted butternut squash, Gruyère, and chopped pecans. Ana's Whipped Goat Cheese with Almonds and Golden Raisins (page 59) would make an amazing topping. ◆ **MAURA**

SERVES 8 TO 10

DATE ORANGE BRIOCHE TART

8 ounces Tahini Brioche Dough (page 29), cold

Dates

½ cup freshly squeezed orange juice

1 cup packed, pitted Medjool dates, chopped

Cheese Filling

Juice and zest from 1 orange

8 ounces mascarpone cheese or cream cheese

Halvah Crumb

¼ cup crumbled halvah (see page 234)

2 tablespoons confectioners' sugar

½ cup all-purpose flour

½ teaspoon kosher salt

1 tablespoon (2 ounces) unsalted butter, chilled and cut into ¼-inch cubes

Line a baking sheet with parchment paper. Butter a 9-inch springform pan and place on the baking sheet. Lightly flour a work surface.

Press the dough into a circle. Place in the prepared pan (it does not have to fill the 9-inch pan; it will expand as it proofs) and cover with plastic wrap. Set aside at room temperature until almost doubled in size, 1½ to 2 hours.

Preheat the oven to 350°F.

To prepare the dates, combine the orange juice and dates in a saucepan. Cook over low heat until dates are softened and a spreadable consistency, 3 to 5 minutes. Remove from the heat and set aside to cool.

To make the cheese filling, combine the orange juice and zest and mascarpone in a small bowl and mix well. Set aside.

To make the halvah crumb, combine the halvah, confectioners' sugar, flour, and salt in a bowl and mix well. Using your hands, mix in the butter until it is in tiny pieces and the mixture is crumbly. Chill the crumb before using.

Once the tahini brioche has proofed, press out the dough to the edges of the pan, dimpling it with your fingertips. Spread an even layer of cheese filling over the top. Add an even layer of cooked dates. Sprinkle the halvah crumb on top.

Place the pan on a baking sheet and bake until the edges are golden brown, 35 to 40 minutes.

Snap off the springform pan and let cool completely on a wire rack. Slice into 8 to 10 pieces to serve.

Turkish legend has it that the first version of asure (pronounced a- shur-a), also known as Noah's pudding, was made by the biblical Noah. After weeks on the ark, as the food supply dwindled, he threw a little of everything he had into one pot. What he got was this delicious pudding that kept everyone well fed until the ark finally rested on Mount Ararak in Turkey. It is considered one of the oldest desserts in the world, but we serve it as a breakfast cereal. Beyaz asure, or white asure, is a version where the grains are cooked in milk instead of water, making it perfect for breakfast. It is also traditionally made with beans, but we have substituted more grains and cooked the pistachios until they have become soft and beanlike in texture. There are no rules with asure; you can play around with any type of grain you like. ◆ **MAURA**

MAKES 6 SERVINGS

ASURE (GRAIN PUDDING)

1 cup hulled barley

½ cup rye berries

1 cup dried chickpeas

4 cups whole milk

½ cup sugar

½ cup shelled raw whole pistachios

2 tablespoons fine-ground bulgur wheat

2 teaspoons rose water

Garnishes: honey, chopped apricots, sliced almonds, chopped Medjool dates, unsweetened shredded coconut, pomegranate seeds

Put the barley, rye berries, and chickpeas in three separate bowls and cover each with 3 cups water. Set aside to soak overnight.

Drain the barley, rye berries, and chickpeas separately. Fill three separate sauce pots with 4 cups water each. Place the barley, rye berries, and chickpeas separately into each of the pots. Bring each to a boil. Cook barley and rye berries until each grain is plumped and softened, 20 to 25 minutes. Drain but do not rinse (the starch will help thicken the milk). Boil the chickpeas for about 40 minutes, until just soft but not falling apart.

Combine the milk and sugar in a large pot and bring to a boil over medium heat. Cook until the sugar is dissolved, about 3 minutes. Add the cooked grains and chickpeas. Lower the heat and simmer until the mixture begins to thicken, 10 to 15 minutes. Add the pistachios and simmer for an additional 10 minutes. Stir in the bulgur and continue cooking until thickened, an additional 5 to 10 minutes.

Remove from the heat and stir in the rose water. Serve warm, garnished with a drizzle of honey and dried fruits and nuts.

COOK'S NOTE Plan ahead. Cooking each grain separately takes a lot of time. Cook larger batches of each grain and freeze. You can thaw them in the refrigerator the night before you plan on making this.

This granola has all the characteristics I look for when developing Sofra recipes: olive oil for a slight savory flavor and date molasses for depth and mild bitterness. Adding our Moroccan Spiced Almonds after baking gives this granola an extra saltiness, which I love. ◆ **MAURA**

MAKES 5 CUPS

OLIVE OIL GRANOLA

3 cups old-fashioned rolled oats

¾ cup golden flax seeds

⅓ cup toasted sesame seeds (see page 241)

¼ cup Demerara sugar or natural cane sugar

2 teaspoons ground cinnamon

1 teaspoon fleur de sel or kosher salt

1 cup golden raisins

¾ cup pitted finely chopped Medjool dates

1½ cups Moroccan Spiced Almonds (page 227)

⅓ cup extra-virgin olive oil

½ cup honey

2 teaspoons date molasses or date syrup (see page 232)

Preheat the oven to 300°F. Line a baking sheet with parchment paper and spray the paper with olive oil cooking spray.

Combine the oats, flax seeds, sesame seeds, Demerara sugar, cinnamon, and fleur de sel in a large bowl.

Combine the raisins, dates, and spiced almonds in a separate bowl; set aside.

Combine the olive oil, honey, and date molasses in a saucepan and whisk over medium heat until combined. Pour the oil mixture into the bowl with the oats. Using a rubber spatula, toss to coat evenly. Spread the mixture on the prepared baking sheet.

Bake for 15 minutes. Stir to break apart and then bake for an additional 15 to 20 minutes, until a toasted brown color.

The granola will not dry during baking but will as it cools. Continue to stir as the granola cools, until the mixture breaks apart. When it has cooled completely, stir in the raisins, dates, and almonds. Store in an airtight container at room temperature for up to 3 weeks.

This is a fun interpretation of the original toaster pastry, Kellogg's Pop-Tarts. The filling is flavored with mastic, a resin from a tree on the island of Chios, Greece, that comes in hard rock crystals that first have to be ground to a powder with a mortar and pestle. Mastic must be used with a very light hand; if used properly, it adds a delicate pine flavor. It's also great added to shortbread cookies, ice creams, and puddings. If you omit the mastic, these tarts are still delicious and unique. Prepare the filling at least one day before making them. The cream cheese dough, which is very simple to prepare and creates flaky layers like puff pastry, needs to chill for 6 to 12 hours before the pastries are assembled. ◆ **MAURA**

MAKES 12

PISTACHIO TOASTER PASTRIES WITH ROSE WATER GLAZE

Pistachio Filling

½ cup white sugar

½ cup water

½ teaspoon ground mastic (see page 237)

1 cup shelled pistachios

Cream Cheese Dough

2 sticks (8 ounces) unsalted butter, chilled and cut into ¼-inch cubes

8 ounces cream cheese, chilled

1½ cups all-purpose flour

Egg Wash

1 egg

2 teaspoons whole milk

Rose Water Glaze

1 cup confectioners' sugar

¼ cup whole milk, plus more as needed

1 teaspoon rose water

Preheat the oven to 350°F.

To make the pistachio filling, combine the sugar, water, and ground mastic in a small saucepan and bring to a boil over high heat. Cook until the sugar is dissolved, about 1 minute. The mastic will make a cloudy film on top, but this will disappear when the filling is processed. Set aside to cool.

Put the pistachios on a baking sheet and bake until lightly toasted, about 8 minutes. Set aside to cool.

Transfer the cooled pistachios to the bowl of a food processor fitted with a steel blade. Process for 10 to 15 seconds and then, with the machine running, pour in the cooled sugar syrup. Transfer to a small container, cover, and refrigerate. The nuts will absorb the syrup as they cool.

To make the cream cheese dough, lightly flour a work surface. Combine the butter, cream cheese, and flour in the bowl of a stand mixer fitted with a paddle attachment. Mix on low speed until the dough comes together, about 4 minutes.

Transfer to the prepared work surface and knead just until smooth; do not overwork. Press the dough into an 8 by 10-inch flat rectangle and divide into two pieces. Wrap each with plastic wrap and refrigerate for at least 6 hours, or up to 4 days.

To assemble the pastries, work with half and refrigerate the other half. Working from the center of the dough and rolling out in each direction, roll the dough into a 10 by 10-inch square. Take the left side of the dough and fold it into the center, then fold the right side over to form a rectangle. Turn the dough 90 degrees. You are giving the dough a tri-fold. Roll the dough into a 10½ by 10½-inch square. Start rolling from the center out in one direction; do not roll in a back-and-forth motion. It is important not to overwork the dough, to prevent it from shrinking. Repeat with the other half.

Working with one sheet of dough while the other remains in the refrigerator, use a ruler to score the dough into 3½ by 3½- inch squares, but do not cut all the way through.

Place 2 tablespoons of the pistachio filling in the center of each scored square. Place the second sheet of dough on top, carefully pressing between the pistachio paste to form squares. Using a ruler, carefully cut into 3½ by 3½-inch squares with a fluted pastry cutter or pizza wheel. Secure the tops to the bottoms by pressing the edges together with a fork. Cover and refrigerate for at least 1 hour, or up to overnight. Pastries can also be frozen for up to 1 month.

Preheat the oven to 350°F. Line a baking sheet with parchment paper.

To make the egg wash, whisk together the egg and milk. Place the pastries on the prepared baking sheet 2 inches apart. Brush with the egg wash. Bake until light golden, 35 minutes. Set aside to cool on the baking sheet. If you have frozen the pastries, thaw them in the refrigerator for at least 2 hours or overnight before baking. Do not thaw them on the counter; it is important that the pastries be baked while they are cold.

Make the rose water glaze while the pastries are cooling. Put the confectioners' sugar in a bowl. Whisk in the milk and rose water. You may need to add additional milk for consistency. Once the pastries are completely cooled, drizzle with the glaze.

When perfect local raspberries start arriving, we immediately make jam for these seasonal turnovers. The Rose Petal Jam adds an extra bit of flavor, turning common turnovers into something truly special. If you don't want to make the jam yourself, you can purchase it from Middle Eastern specialty shops ◆ **MAURA**

MAKES 9

RASPBERRY–ROSE PETAL TURNOVERS

Cream Cheese Dough

2 sticks (8 ounces) unsalted butter, chilled and cut into ¼-inch cubes

8 ounces cream cheese, chilled

1½ cups all-purpose flour

Egg Wash

1 egg

2 teaspoons whole milk

Raspberry Rose Filling

2 cups fresh raspberries

2 tablespoons raspberry jam

1 tablespoon Rose Petal Jam (page 226)

1 tablespoon cornstarch

Sanding sugar or granulated sugar

To make the cream cheese dough, lightly flour a work surface. Combine the butter, cream cheese, and flour in the bowl of a stand mixer fitted with a paddle attachment. Mix on low speed until the dough comes together. Turn out onto the prepared work surface and knead just until smooth. Press flat and roll into a 10 by 16-inch rectangle. Wrap in plastic wrap and refrigerate overnight. The dough can be made up to 3 days in advance.

Lightly flour a work surface. Roll the dough into a 10 by 10-inch square. First fold the left side of the dough over into the center, then fold the right side over to form a rectangle. Turn the rectangle 90 degrees. You are giving the dough a tri-fold. Start rolling from the center out in each direction until you have a 12 by 12-inch square. It is important not to overwork the dough or it will shrink. Use a pizza cutter and cut into 4 by 4-inch squares. Place the squares on a baking sheet. Cover and refrigerate for at least 1 hour. The squares can be made up to 4 days in advance and kept refrigerated.

To make the egg wash, whisk together the egg and milk.

To make the filling, in a large bowl, gently toss together the raspberries, raspberry jam, Rose Petal Jam, and cornstarch.

Take the dough out of the refrigerator. Place 1 tablespoon of the raspberry filling in the center of a pastry square. Brush two sides lightly with the egg wash, then fold the dough over to form a triangle, leaving a ½-inch border, firmly pressing it together to seal. Crimp the edges with a fork to seal. Repeat with the remaining squares. Refrigerate for at least 1 hour, or up to overnight.

Preheat the oven to 350°F. Brush the top of each turnover with the remaining egg wash. Cut two small slits in the center of each. Sprinkle the sugar on top. Place on a prepared baking sheet 2 inches apart. Bake until golden brown and crisp at the edges, 30 to 35 minutes. Set aside to cool on the baking sheet.

Serve warm or at room temperature.

Traditional simit (sesame-coated bread rings) are beloved breads sold from street vendors everywhere in Turkey. They have the perfect ratio of crunchy crust to chewy center, similar to a bagel. The crispiness, coming from grape molasses (pekmez), is unique to simit. When I'm in Istanbul, I look for the red cart of fresh simit or for the "Simit Man" walking around with a tray of simit on his head, for this daily treat. A simit is great to tear apart and enjoy while walking the streets or as part of your Turkish breakfast. One of the most common ways to eat it is to dip it into tahini, which makes it taste just like peanut butter and jelly. ◆ **MAURA**

MAKES 10 BREAD RINGS

TURKISH SIMIT

1½ cups room-temperature water

1 tablespoon active dry yeast

1 tablespoon sugar

3⅓ cups all-purpose flour

1½ teaspoons kosher salt

1½ cups sesame seeds, toasted (see page 241)

½ cup grape molasses (pekmez) (see note below and page 233)

PEKMEZ Available at Middle Eastern stores, pekmez is grape molasses. Brush it on with a very light touch—"just kiss the dough," as our good friend in Istanbul suggests. For an authentic simit with a light caramel and crunchy crust, there is no substitute for pekmez. It's found in Turkish homes and used the way we use granulated sugar. It is common for moms to give their kids a spoonful of pekmez each morning; it helps in blood circulation and rejuvenation.

In the bowl of a stand mixer fitted with a whisk attachment, combine ¼ cup of the water, yeast, and sugar. Set aside until frothy, 5 minutes.

Add the flour, salt, and remaining 1¼ cups water. Using a dough hook, mix on medium-low speed until a smooth elastic dough is formed, 8 to 10 minutes. Scrape down the sides of the bowl and form the dough into a ball. Return the dough to the bowl and cover with plastic wrap. Leave the dough out until doubled in size, about 1 hour.

Preheat the oven to 425°F. Line a baking sheet with parchment paper. Lightly flour a work surface.

Punch down the dough in the bowl. Transfer to the work surface and press out into a flat rectangle, 12 by 4 inches. With the shorter side facing you, cut across the dough, dividing the dough into 10 even strips.

Fold each strip in half and gently stretch it out as you twist it into a rope. Join the ends together to form a circle like a twisted bagel. Place on the prepared baking. Repeat with the remaining dough.

Put the sesame seeds on a large plate. Dip a brush into the pekmez and dab each simit very lightly. Then lift each piece and invert it onto the sesame seeds to completely coat the surface. Return to the baking sheet, placing the simit 2 inches apart. Set aside at room temperature to proof for an 15 additional minutes.

Bake until golden brown, 20 to 25 minutes. Serve immediately or set aside to cool on the baking sheet.

This popular treat was one of the first recipes I developed for Sofra. It started when I used the orange blossom glaze on a dessert at Oleana, and I knew I had to find a home for it at our upcoming bakery. The bun is a sugary pull-apart yeasted muffin. When we opened, we made croissants daily and we used the scrap pieces for these. Now, we only make croissant dough to cut it up into pieces for our Morning Buns. This is a time-consuming recipe, but this book would not be complete without it. It is necessary to start this dough at least two days in advance. Once the butter is incorporated and cubes are cut, it is best if you refrigerate the cubes overnight. The dough can also be frozen for up to four days. ◆ **MAURA**

MAKES 12

MORNING BUNS WITH ORANGE BLOSSOM GLAZE

1¼ cups whole milk, at room temperature

2½ teaspoons active dry yeast

¾ cup granulated sugar

2¾ cups all-purpose flour

½ teaspoon kosher salt

2 tablespoons (1 ounce) unsalted butter, chilled and cut into ¼-inch cubes

2 sticks (8 ounces) unsalted butter, at room temperature

2 teaspoons ground cinnamon

½ teaspoon ground cardamom

1 egg

Orange Blossom Glaze

1 cup confectioners' sugar

¼ cup freshly squeezed orange juice (from about 2 large oranges)

2 teaspoons orange blossom water

2 tablespoons grated orange zest

Lightly flour a work surface.

Combine the milk and yeast in the bowl of a stand mixer and whisk well by hand. Add ¼ cup of the granulated sugar, the flour, and salt. Add the cubed butter and, using a dough hook, mix on low speed until a soft dough forms, 2 to 3 minutes. Transfer the dough to the work surface and finish kneading by hand until it forms a smooth, soft ball.

Line a baking sheet with parchment paper. Lightly dust it with flour and place the ball of dough on it . Cut two slits 1 inch deep into the ball in an X pattern. Wrap the baking sheet with plastic wrap and refrigerate overnight.

Put the room-temperature butter in the bowl of a stand mixer fitted with a paddle attachment and mix on low speed until smooth. Scrape the butter onto a piece of parchment or plastic wrap and shape into a 6 by 8-inch rectangle. Wrap in parchment paper or plastic wrap and refrigerate overnight.

The next day, remove the butter block from the refrigerator to soften for 15 for 20 minutes before starting to roll out the buns. It is important that the butter and the dough have similar consistencies.

Lightly flour a work surface.

Put the dough on the prepared work surface. Roll the dough into a 10-inch square. Unwrap the butter and place in the center of the dough. Starting with the left side, fold the dough over the butter, stretching it slightly if needed to reach the center of the butter;

> > >

MORNING BUNS WITH
ORANGE BLOSSOM GLAZE

repeat with the other corners of the dough to completely enclose the butter block. Take your rolling pin and gently press down on the top. It is very important to seal in the butter completely.

Turn the dough 90 degrees. Roll the dough into a 12 by 10-inch rectangle. Brush off the excess flour. Take the left side of the dough and fold it into the center, then take the right side and fold it into the center to form a rectangle. This is the first tri-fold.

Roll the dough again into a 12 by 10-inch rectangle. Brush off the excess flour and fold the dough into thirds again. Put the dough back on the baking sheet and refrigerate for 30 minutes.

Lightly flour a work surface. Roll the dough with the sealed end to the left side, into a 12 by 10-inch rectangle. This time, fold the left side of the dough into the center. Fold the right side to meet the left edge in the center, then fold the left side over; this final turn is a bookfold. Rotate the dough 90 degrees. Roll the dough out into a 12 by 10-inch rectangle. Brush off excess flour. Fold the dough into thirds this time. Place on the prepared baking sheet. Wrap in plastic wrap and refrigerate for 3 hours.

Lightly flour a work surface. Place the chilled dough on the prepared work surface. Roll the dough to ¼-inch thickness and, using a pizza cutter, cut into ½-inch squares. Place the dough in a sealed container and refrigerate for at least 4 hours, or up to overnight. Squares can be frozen for 4 days and thawed in the refrigerator the night before you plan to prepare the buns.

In a small bowl, combine the remaining ½ cup granulated sugar, cinnamon, and cardamom. In a large bowl, whisk the egg and toss the cubed dough into the egg to break it apart and coat each cube. Sprinkle the spiced sugar in and toss to coat completely.

Spray a standard muffin pan with nonstick cooking spray, making sure to spray the portion of the pan between the cups, because the buns will expand. Place a standard muffin paper liner in each.

Fill each paper liner with sugared dough, about 12 cubes per muffin. Press down firmly. Cover the entire pan with plastic wrap and let rise at room temperature for 1½ to 2 hours. The dough will be soft and puffy when touched.

Preheat the oven to 350°F.

Place the muffin pan on a baking sheet and bake until the buns are puffed and golden in color, 35 minutes. Cool completely in the pan before glazing.

To make the glaze, sift the confectioners' sugar into a bowl. Whisk in orange juice, orange blossom water, and orange zest until the glaze has a smooth, thick consistency. Place a generous spoonful on each morning bun. These buns are best served the day they are made.

MEZE

Throughout the Eastern Mediterranean and Middle East, meze is a common way to start a meal. Like Spain's tapas, many small plates of food are shared with family and friends for a variety of small tastes. The point of eating this way is to make the experience at the table last as long as possible, allowing time to sip and share thoughts. Traditional meze often include vegetables, cheeses, yogurt, salads, nuts, and grains. Spice and herb combinations are the secret to giving these little dishes their big flavors without making them heavy. We've learned that when we eat this way, we fill up on a lot of vegetables. If you start with meze and lead into a richer meat or protein course, you often need less to be satisfied. It's a healthy, social, and delicious way to cook and eat.

All the recipes in this chapter are designed to be mixed and matched. Make a meal out of three meze or serve as many as ten for an elaborate meal. Meze can also be served as a side dish to an entrée of chicken, lamb, or beef.

On Ana's first trip to Turkey, her friend Ayfer Unsal and her friends graciously threw a welcome lunch, potluck-style, in the park. Everyone—including Ana—prepared a favorite recipe. There were thirty perfected meze dishes spread out from one end of the table to the other. Ana tasted every single one and marveled at how rich and complex the flavors were, essentially making her way through a thirty-course tasting menu without ending up too full. This is the idea behind meze—many dishes that together make a meal.

One of my favorite crops from my husband's farm are his fall carrots. I prefer the fall carrots because as the weather gets colder the vegetable sugars concentrate, yielding the sweetest carrots of the year. We use lots of carrots in this recipe, so that it's more about the carrots than anything else. For the best flavor, serve it cold the day after you make it. You can substitute chickpeas for the black-eyed peas, if you prefer to use another type of bean. ◆ **ANA**

SERVES 6 TO 8

PERSIAN-STYLE CARROTS AND BLACK-EYED PEAS

1 cup dried black-eyed peas

½ teaspoon kosher salt, plus more to taste

Pinch of saffron

2 tablespoons warm tap water

2 tablespoons extra-virgin olive oil

1 small onion, finely chopped

4 cups thin carrot rounds

1 red bell pepper, stemmed, seeded, and finely chopped

1½ teaspoons Persian Spice (page 218)

1 teaspoon finely chopped garlic

Freshly ground black pepper

1 teaspoon freshly squeezed lemon juice

2 teaspoons honey

2 tablespoons chopped fresh flat-leaf parsley leaves

In a medium-sized saucepan, combine the black-eyed peas and 4 cups water and bring to a boil over high heat. Lower the heat and simmer until tender, about 25 minutes. Off the heat, add the salt and set aside while the peas absorb some salt for 10 minutes. Drain.

Meanwhile, put the saffron and water in a small bowl. Mix and set aside for at least 15 minutes and as long as overnight.

Place a large sauté pan over medium-low heat and add the olive oil, onion, carrots, and red bell pepper, stirring until the peppers start to soften and the onion is translucent, about 10 minutes. Add the saffron (and its blooming water), Persian Spice, garlic, and black-eyed peas. Season the carrots and peas with salt and pepper to taste and stew until the carrots and peppers are tender and the black-eyed peas are glazed.

Remove from the heat and set aside to cool. Stir in the lemon juice, honey, and parsley. Serve cold or at room temperature.

Labne is yogurt that has been wrapped in cheesecloth and allowed to drain for a few days, resulting in a yogurt that is thick enough for a spoon to stand up in. This hot pepper labne is delicious eaten with pita bread or served as a sauce for grilled meats or vegetables. We love it by the spoonful and prefer to make this with Hungarian wax peppers because they are spicy but not too hot. You can buy commercially made labne in many Middle Eastern, Greek, and Armenian markets. ◆ **ANA**

MAKES 1½ CUPS; SERVES 4 TO 6

HOT PEPPER LABNE

4 Hungarian wax peppers

1 tablespoon extra-virgin olive oil

½ teaspoon kosher salt, plus more to taste

1 teaspoon finely chopped garlic

1 tablespoon freshly squeezed lemon juice

1½ cups labne (page 233)

Preheat the oven to 350°F.

Combine the peppers, oil, and salt in a mixing bowl and toss until coated. Transfer the peppers to a heavy baking sheet, and roast until the peppers blister and collapse, about 8 minutes on each side.

When the peppers are cool enough to handle, remove the stems and scrape away any bits of waxy skin where possible. (The seeds are the best part so don't get rid of them!) Finely chop the peppers until they form a coarse paste.

Put the garlic and lemon juice in a small mixing bowl and set aside until the garlic is lightly pickled, 3 to 5 minutes. Add the labne and ½ cup of the roasted pepper paste and stir well. Depending on the size (and heat) of the Hungarian wax peppers, you may yield ½ cup or have a little left over. If you have left over, you can taste to see if you want the labne spicier and add more, or you can cover the surface of the peppers with a little olive oil and keep them on hand in the refrigerator to add to eggs, soup, or any dish to give it a little kick. Add salt to taste. Serve immediately cold or at room temperature or cover and refrigerate for up to 5 days.

COOK'S NOTE You can also roast the peppers in a pan: Heat a large cast-iron pan on the stove over medium-high heat with 1 teaspoon of olive oil. Add the peppers and cook until they blister and collapse, 3 to 4 minutes on each side.

Inspired by bisarra, a fava bean puree and salad from Egypt, this is the perfect salad to make in the spring or early summer when fresh shelling peas are available. I like to coarsely chop the peas until they just start sticking together rather than making a smooth puree or leaving them whole. This way, the flavors marry better and the salad comes together when you pick it up with the spoon. I like it best spooned on toasted bread. ◆ **ANA**

SERVES 4

EGYPTIAN-STYLE PEA SALAD WITH WALNUTS

1 teaspoon kosher salt, plus more to taste

2 cups shelled green peas, fresh or frozen

2 tablespoons extra-virgin olive oil

¼ cup finely chopped shallots or green onions, mostly the white part

½ teaspoon finely chopped garlic

2 tablespoons coarsely chopped fresh flat-leaf parsley leaves

2 tablespoons coarsely chopped fresh spearmint leaves

2 tablespoons coarsely chopped fresh dill leaves

2 tablespoons coarsely chopped fresh cilantro leaves

2 tablespoons walnut oil

Grated zest of 1 lemon

¼ teaspoon Maras pepper (see page 236)

½ cup lightly toasted walnuts, coarsely chopped

In a saucepan, bring 4 cups water to a boil over high heat and add the salt. Add the peas, lower the heat, and simmer until tender, about 4 minutes. If using frozen, let them thaw on a baking sheet for 20 minutes or until they are tender—there is no need to blanch them. Drain immediately and run under cold water to cool down the peas. Roll them around on a paper towel to get them as dry as possible.

Meanwhile, place a small sauté pan over low heat, add 2 teaspoons of the olive oil and the shallots, and sweat the shallots until tender and translucent, about 3 minutes, adding 1 tablespoon water to the pan while they cook to steam and prevent them from browning. Off the heat, stir in the garlic.

Combine the peas, shallot mixture, fresh herbs, the remaining 4 teaspoons olive oil, walnut oil, lemon zest, and Maras pepper in a food processor fitted with a metal blade and pulse until the peas are just sticking together. Season with salt to taste.

Serve with walnuts on top or stir the nuts into the salad. Serve at room temperature or cold. The salad will keep overnight covered in the fridge.

COOK'S NOTE When cooking vegetables to soften them but not to color them, don't bother getting the oil hot before they go in the pan. Extreme heat breaks down the olive oil, and the flavor of the oil is lost. Throughout the book you will find instructions to add vegetables and oil to a pan that isn't hot and that is because we are cooking them to soften, sweat, and sauté instead of to sear or brown them. I prefer gentle heat for this process because it brings out the best in the olive oil and the vegetables.

Plaki is an Armenian, Turkish, and Greek word for a stew that can be eaten warm or cold. Typically, a bean plaki is made with giant white lima beans called gigantes. The beans are first cooked and then stewed in a fresh tomato sauce until the tomato coats the beans like a thick dressing or glaze. In the summer, my husband, farmer Chris Kurth, grows amazing fresh wax beans called dragon's tongue. These are wide, flat, juicy, and speckled with purple spots. They are similar in shape to Romano beans, which are a fine substitute. I like to make plaki with fresh beans and add other vegetables like corn and sweet peppers. Variations of plaki are served warm or cold as a meze on the menus at Sofra, Oleana, and our third restaurant, Sarma. When corn and dragon's tongue beans are not in season, we use cooked gigantes or Peruvian limas and make the traditional version. You'll want to make a big batch of this to have on hand for the week. Simply serve with a chunk of feta and it's a perfect quick meal. ◆ **ANA**

SERVES 8

DRAGON BEAN PLAKI

¼ cup extra-virgin olive oil

1 small summer onion, such as Ailsa Craig or Vidalia, finely chopped

1 carrot, peeled and diced small

1 small (or half of 1 large) green bell pepper, stemmed, seeded, and diced small

1 teaspoon finely chopped garlic

3 cups dragon's tongue beans or other wax beans, cut into ½-inch pieces

3 cups fresh, in-season sweet corn kernels (from about 3 cobs)

6 plum tomatoes, halved

2 teaspoons tomato paste

1 bay leaf

1 tablespoon chopped fresh dill or tarragon leaves

1 teaspoon sherry vinegar

1 teaspoon freshly squeezed lemon juice

Kosher salt and freshly ground black pepper

Place a large deep-sided sauté pan over medium-low heat and add 2 tablespoons of the olive oil. Add the onion, carrot, and bell pepper and sauté until they begin to soften and the onion is translucent, about 8 minutes. Stir in the garlic, beans, and corn and continue to cook until they start to soften, about 10 minutes.

Meanwhile, using your fingers, scrape as many seeds out of the cavities of the tomato as you can without being too fussy. Over a mixing bowl, use the large holes of a box grater to grate the tomatoes (holding the cut side of the tomato to the grater) until you have nothing but skin left in your hand and the flesh of the tomato is in the bowl. Stir the grated tomatoes into the corn mixture and add the remaining 2 tablespoons of olive oil, the tomato paste, and the bay leaf.

Cook until the mixture has thickened and become jamlike, about 20 minutes on low heat. The tomato sauce should coat and cling to the beans and the corn. Pour the plaki into a large mixing bowl and cool to room temperature.

Remove the bay leaf and stir in the dill, vinegar, and lemon juice and season with 1 teaspoon of salt and freshly ground pepper to taste. Serve at room temperature or cold. This salad can easily be made a day or two before serving; the flavors become better overnight. Store it covered in the refrigerator up to 4 days.

Didem Hosgel is our talented chef de cuisine at Sofra. She and I collaborated on this recipe to create a grain and legume salad for a quick-grab lunch. Barley is one of our favorite whole grains, and we are lucky enough to have access to barley grown nearby at Four Star Farms. Other fall vegetables like cabbage or golden beets can be used as a substitute or in addition to the carrots, depending on your preference or the season. Barrel-aged Greek feta is the way to go here because it's more crumbly than the creamy French-style (which I prefer for other recipes). The combination of chopped fresh parsley, mint, and dill is a staple in our kitchen (affectionately referred to as PMD at Sofra) and is used in many different meze and fresh salads. ◆ **ANA**

SERVES 8

BARLEY AND CHICKPEA SALAD

½ cup dried chickpeas

¾ cup hulled or pearl barley

1 bay leaf

¼ cup extra-virgin olive oil

1 cup grated carrots
(about 1 large)

¼ cup golden raisins

2 cups spinach or Swiss chard leaves, cut into thin ribbons

Kosher salt and freshly ground black pepper

3 to 4 ounces crumbled barrel-aged Greek feta

¼ cup finely chopped green onion, mostly the white part

2 tablespoons finely chopped fresh flat parsley leaves

2 tablespoons finely chopped fresh spearmint leaves

2 tablespoons finely chopped fresh dill leaves

¼ cup plain whole-milk yogurt (not Greek)

¾ teaspoon ground cumin

1 teaspoon dried spearmint

1 teaspoon dried oregano

½ teaspoon Maras pepper (see page 236)

1 tablespoon freshly squeezed lemon juice

Grated zest of 1 lemon

Put the chickpeas and 4 cups cold water in a bowl and soak overnight. Drain.

Put the chickpeas in one saucepan and the barley in another. Cover each with 4 cups water and add the bay leaf to the chickpeas. Bring both pots to a boil over high heat. Lower the heat to a simmer and cook until both are tender, skimming off any foam that might come to the surface during the cooking. The barley should take about 25 minutes if you are using pearled and about 40 minutes if you are using hulled. The chickpeas should take 40 to 45 minutes, depending on the size and the age of the chickpeas. Drain and set aside to cool to room temperature. Remove the bay leaf. This can be done the day before.

Meanwhile, place a sauté pan over medium-low heat and add 1 tablespoon olive oil. Add the carrots and sweat until just tender, about 5 minutes. Off the heat, stir in the raisins and spinach. The residual heat from the mixture and the pan will wilt the spinach just a little.

Combine the barley, carrot mixture, and chickpeas in a large mixing bowl and add 1 teaspoon of salt and freshly ground pepper to taste. Add the crumbled feta, green onion, parsley, fresh mint, and dill.

In a small mixing bowl, combine the yogurt, cumin, dried spearmint, oregano, Maras pepper, lemon juice and lemon zest, and remaining 3 tablespoons of olive oil and whisk until you have a thin emulsified dressing. Dress the salad and serve at room temperature or cold. Store covered in the refrigerator up to 4 days.

Inspired by the traditional Greek dish known as htipiti, a blend of creamy feta and sweet roasted peppers, we've made it irresistible by adding Turkish red pepper paste and two different kinds of pepper flakes. The Turkish red pepper paste adds umami flavor and is the hook, line, and sinker for this dish. If you purchase a big jar of the paste, divide it into half-cup portions and pack it into zip-top plastic bags to freeze so that it will last as long as you need it to. I use French feta in this recipe (even though, according to the Greek feta laws, it's not technically feta!) because it's creamier and results in a smoother puree. ◆ **ANA**

SERVES 4

WHIPPED FETA WITH SWEET AND HOT PEPPERS

12 ounces (about 2 cups) crumbled goat milk or sheep's milk feta

2 teaspoons Turkish red pepper paste (see page 244)

¼ cup extra-virgin olive oil

4 piquillo peppers (canned or jarred, roasted, small sweet peppers from Spain)

1 teaspoon freshly squeezed lemon juice

1 teaspoon Maras pepper (see page 236)

2 pinches of smoked salt

2 teaspoons Urfa pepper flakes (see note below and page 245)

Combine the feta, red pepper paste, olive oil, piquillo peppers, lemon juice, Maras pepper, and smoked salt in a food processor fitted with a metal blade. Use the pulse button to blend until smooth and very creamy. Do not overblend; if the mixture is overprocessed, it will separate or have a liquid or runny consistency. Spoon the feta into a serving bowl and sprinkle with Urfa pepper. Serve at room temperature or cold with bread or raw vegetables. Store covered in the refrigerator up to 4 days.

URFA PEPPER Try to find Urfa pepper flakes, the ancho chile of the Middle East, from the Urfa region in southern Turkey. We love it for its deep, complex chocolaty flavor. You will fall in love with both the Urfa and the Maras red pepper flakes and find yourself sprinkling them on almost everything you cook.

Whipped goat cheese makes a perfect tangy and creamy base for toasted almonds, golden raisins, and fresh herbs. I place a spoonful of this mixture onto a radish or arugula salad or spread it onto a thick piece of grilled bread. Try dropping a spoonful into a bowl of hot carrot soup or using it as a first layer on avocado toast in the morning. ◆ **ANA**

SERVES 4 TO 6

WHIPPED GOAT CHEESE WITH ALMONDS AND GOLDEN RAISINS

¼ cup golden raisins

8 ounces soft, creamy fresh goat cheese

¼ cup finely minced red onion or green onion, mostly the white part

1 teaspoon freshly squeezed lemon juice

¼ cup coarsely chopped cilantro leaves

1 tablespoon olive oil

½ cup sliced almonds, lightly toasted

Kosher salt and freshly ground black pepper

Put the raisins in a small heatproof mixing bowl and plump them by pouring boiling water over them until covered. Set aside for 2 minutes, then drain.

Combine the raisins, goat cheese, onion, lemon juice, cilantro, olive oil, and almonds in a mixing bowl and stir until the mixture is a little creamy and the ingredients are whipped into the cheese. Season with salt and freshly ground black pepper to taste. Serve at room temperature or cold with crackers, flatbreads, salad greens, or raw vegetables. Store covered in the refrigerator up to 4 days.

The ingredients for a spoon salad are chopped small so that they can be eaten with a spoon or on a leaf of romaine. Spoon salads remind me of traditional Spanish gazpachos in which, as the vegetables sit, they weep a beautiful clean vegetable juice that is delicious to slurp up or soak into pita bread. There is a lot of opportunity to create different colors and textures in this salad by using yellow or orange peppers or a variety of heirloom tomatoes that might be in season in the early fall. If fresh pomegranates aren't available, you can leave them out or substitute finely chopped French breakfast or watermelon radishes. If it's summertime and hot, you can stir some ice cubes into the salad to quickly chill it and encourage more juices to form from the vegetables. It is delicious as is or served with yogurt, fried peppers, or grilled fish. ◆ **ANA**

SERVES 4 TO 6

SPOON SALAD

1 pound plum tomatoes, seeded and finely chopped (about 2 cups)

1 small red onion, minced, or ½ cup finely chopped green onions, mostly the white part

1 Persian or ½ large English cucumber, halved, seeded, and diced small (about 1 cup)

1 small green bell pepper, stemmed, seeded, and diced small (about ½ cup)

6 tablespoons extra-virgin olive oil

1½ tablespoons freshly squeezed lemon juice

1 tablespoon pomegranate molasses (see page 240)

½ cup pomegranate seeds (about ½ pomegranate)

1 tablespoon chopped fresh flat-leaf parsley leaves

2 tablespoons chopped fresh spearmint leaves

1 tablespoon chopped fresh dill leaves

1 teaspoon Maras pepper (see page 236)

Kosher salt and freshly ground black pepper

8 romaine lettuce leaves, torn into large pieces

Place the tomatoes in a fine sieve over a bowl and add ¼ teaspoon of salt. Stir and let the water drain from the tomatoes for about 10 minutes.

Combine the onion, cucumber, green bell pepper, olive oil, lemon juice, pomegranate molasses, pomegranate seeds, parsley, mint, dill, and Maras pepper in a bowl. Stir in the drained tomatoes. Season with salt and pepper to taste.

Serve at room temperature or chilled with the romaine leaves to scoop up the salad. The salad is best eaten the day it's made but it can be covered and stored overnight in the refrigerator.

Cacik is a Turkish yogurt meze—somewhat like a dip, somewhat like a salad—made with cucumber and dried mint. It is very similar to the better-known Greek tzatziki, in which oregano is used in place of mint. At Sofra, we make cacik with loads of other vegetables and herbs in addition to cucumber. The only rule is that they must be green! Cacik makes a great meze served on top of pita bread or, as we often do, on top of Za'atar Bread with finely shredded and lightly dressed romaine lettuce. It's also fabulous used as a sauce for grilled chicken or lamb or served with thick potato chips for dipping. ◆ **ANA**

SERVES 6

CACIK

Kosher salt

12 ounces spinach, stemmed

1 teaspoon finely chopped garlic

1 tablespoon freshly squeezed lemon juice

2 cups plain whole-milk Greek yogurt

Freshly ground black pepper

¼ cup finely chopped green onions, mostly the white part

½ cup shelled green peas, blanched (optional, when in season)

1 Persian cucumber or ⅓ English cucumber, split in half, seeded, and diced small

2 tablespoons chopped fresh flat-leaf parsley leaves

1½ teaspoons dried spearmint

1 tablespoon chopped fresh spearmint leaves

1 tablespoon chopped fresh dill leaves

¼ cup extra-virgin olive oil

4 romaine leaves, cut into thin ribbons

1 teaspoon Maras pepper (see page 236)

Pita bread, potato chips, Za'atar Bread (page 114), or grilled meats, to serve

Bring a pot of water to a boil over high heat. Add 1 tablespoon salt and the spinach and cook until the spinach is softened, about 2 minutes. Drain immediately and run cold water over it until cool enough to handle. Squeeze the water out by picking up small handfuls and squeezing as hard as you can between the palms of your hands. You should end up with ⅓ to ½ cup. Finely chop the spinach.

In a bowl, stir the garlic and the lemon juice until combined. Sprinkle with a pinch of salt and let stand for about 5 minutes to lightly pickle the garlic.

Stir in the yogurt and season with 1¾ teaspoons salt and pepper to taste. Add the spinach, green onions, peas, cucumber, parsley, fresh mint, dill, dried mint, and 2 tablespoons olive oil and stir until everything is coated with the thick yogurt.

Toss the thinly sliced romaine with 1 tablespoon of the olive oil and season with salt to taste.

Serve the cacik in a bowl and make a well in the center of it using the back of a spoon. Pour the remaining 1 tablespoon olive oil into the well and sprinkle with the Maras pepper. Top with the romaine and serve at room temperature or cold with pita bread, potato chips, za'atar bread, or grilled meats. Store covered in the refrigerator up to 2 days.

A monk lives a frugal life, eating whatever vegetables his plot of land produces. This salad could be anything freshly harvested from the monk's garden and is one of my all-time favorite summer and early fall meze when our eggplants are at their best. It reminds me of guacamole because it has that same rich, velvety texture. I prefer to use long, thin, lavender-colored Asian eggplants because they are white, fluffy, creamy, and never bitter. Have some fun with the variety of other vegetables and swap cucumber for fennel or add some hot peppers in place of some of the green bell peppers. I garnish this dish with Urfa pepper, which is one of my favorite spices to use on eggplant because of its lightly smoked flavor and rich, earthy heat. ◆ **ANA**

SERVES 6

MONK'S SALAD

2¾ teaspoons kosher salt, plus more to taste

1½ pounds eggplant (1 large Italian globe eggplant or 4 to 5 long, narrow Asian eggplants)

1 teaspoon finely chopped garlic

2 tablespoons freshly squeezed lemon juice

¼ cup extra-virgin olive oil

1 tablespoon pomegranate molasses (see page 240)

2 beefsteak or heirloom tomatoes, cut in small dice

1 cup chopped fresh cilantro leaves

½ cup finely chopped green onions, mostly the white part (or finely chopped sweet onion)

1 small green bell pepper, seeded, cored, and diced small

½ cup finely chopped fennel bulb (about ½ bulb)

2 teaspoons Urfa pepper flakes (see page 245)

Bring a large pot of water to a boil and add 2 teaspoons salt.

Meanwhile, trim the green caps off the eggplant by pulling them up towards the top of the eggplant so that all you have left is the stem. Trim the stem off. Peel and cut the eggplant into 2-inch chunks.

Cook the eggplant in the boiling water until the eggplant is tender when squeezed with a pair of tongs, 10 to 12 minutes. Drain immediately and set aside to cool. You should have about 4 cups cooked eggplant.

Meanwhile, in a large mixing bowl, let the minced garlic sit in lemon juice for at least 5 minutes to soften the raw flavor.

Add the eggplant to the garlic and, using a whisk, mix until broken up and little creamy. Whisk in the olive oil and pomegranate molasses. Add the tomatoes, cilantro, green onions, green bell pepper, and fennel. Season to taste with about ¾ teaspoon salt. Garnish with Urfa pepper flakes and serve at room temperature or cold with pita, grilled meats, salad greens, or a chunk of feta. Store covered in the refrigerator up to 3 days.

COOK'S NOTE When tomatoes aren't looking their best, you can substitute 1 cup finely chopped blanched green beans or 1 cup super-fresh, raw sweet corn kernels.

Called kisir in Turkey, this salad derives its power from delicious, ripe, in-season tomatoes. Coarsely grate the tomatoes for their pulp, then whisk in a red pepper paste made with sweet and hot peppers and olive oil. Then add finely milled bulgur wheat to thicken it and you have a Turkish version of panzanella! The whole-grain bulgur swells and absorbs all the flavor and juices of the tomato and remains lighter than a bread salad. The color is red but it may remind you of tabbouleh because of the bulgur. However, the texture is more dumpling-like because you can pick it up and eat it with your fingers as you could a bread salad. I like to serve it with peeled and hollowed-out heirloom tomato halves stuffed with labne. The salad is also a delicious platform for pure, simple slices of a perfect, vine-ripened heirloom tomato. Make it as spicy as you like by adding more Maras pepper flakes. ◆ **ANA**

SERVES 6 TO 8

SPICY TOMATO AND BULGUR SALAD

2 to 3 large heirloom tomatoes, halved

1 small green bell pepper, stemmed, seeded, and diced small (about ½ cup)

½ red bell pepper, stemmed, seeded, and diced small (about ½ cup)

1 bunch green onions, mostly the white part, finely chopped (about ¾ cup)

1 tablespoon Turkish red pepper paste (see page 244)

1 tablespoon tomato paste

1½ teaspoons ground cumin

1½ teaspoons Maras pepper (see page 236)

¾ cup extra-virgin olive oil

Kosher salt

2 cups fine-ground bulgur wheat

8 romaine leaves

½ cup pickled pepperoncini or other pickled hot peppers, stems removed

Using your fingers, scrape as many seeds out of the cavities of the tomatoes as you can without being too fussy. Over a large mixing bowl, use the large holes of a box grater to grate the tomato (holding the cut side of the tomato to the grater) until you have nothing but skin left in your hand and the flesh of the tomato is in the bowl. It should measure 2 cups.

Combine the tomato, green and red bell peppers, green onions, red pepper paste, tomato paste, cumin, and Maras pepper in a mixing bowl and whisk until combined. Stir in the olive oil to make a shiny vinaigrette. Season with 1 teaspoon salt or to taste.

Stir in the bulgur and mix well. Set aside until the bulgur has swelled and absorbed the liquid from the tomato, about 10 minutes. Knead the mixture with a wooden spoon until it seems a little fluffier and stays together when squeezed in your hand, 3 to 4 minutes.

Serve at room temperature or cold with lettuce leaves and hot pickled peppers on the side. Use the lettuce leaves to scoop up the salad and top each bite with a pickled pepper. Store covered in the refrigerator for up to 3 days.

Our house-made crackers are known as crick cracks, a name invented by Ayfer Unsal, a mentor of Ana's from her first trip to Turkey. This recipe originally appeared in Ana's book, *Spice*, but since Sofra opened, these crackers have been our most popular item. After almost fifteen years of creating plated desserts at Oleana and cookies, pies, and pastries here at Sofra, this is the recipe I am most proud of. Creating the perfect cracker was a big challenge, but the result is irresistible. This dough also can be turned into a quick tart shell for the Cheese and Honey Fatayer (page 138). ◆ **MAURA**

MAKES 1 POUND OF CRACKERS, APPROXIMATELY 3 DOZEN, TO SERVE WITH MEZE

CRICK CRACKS

Dough

1½ cups all-purpose flour, plus ½ to ¾ cup for rolling out the dough

¾ cup yellow cornmeal

1 tablespoon sugar

1½ teaspoons kosher salt

1¼ sticks (5 ounces) unsalted butter, chilled and cut into ¼-inch cubes

¾ cup buttermilk

Topping

2 tablespoons sesame seeds, toasted (see page 241)

2 tablespoons nigella seeds (see page 237)

¼ cup water

To make the dough, combine 1½ cups flour, ½ cup of the cornmeal, the sugar, ½ teaspoon of the salt, and the butter in a stand mixer fitted with a paddle attachment. Mix on low speed until the butter breaks down to almost invisible pieces; the mixture will resemble sand. Add the buttermilk. The dough will come together quickly and be quite wet.

Lightly flour a work surface. Transfer the dough to the work surface and form it into a flat rectangle approximately 8 by 4 inches and about 1 inch thick. Wrap in plastic and refrigerate overnight.

Divide the dough into quarters. Lightly flour a work surface. Roll out the first quarter of the dough into a rectangle approximately 12 inches by 14 inches and ⅟₁₆ inch thick. Don't worry about rolling the dough into a perfect rectangle; it is more important that it rolls out to the perfect thickness.

Line a baking sheet with parchment paper and sprinkle lightly with 1 tablespoon of cornmeal. Carefully lift the rolled sheet of dough and place on the prepared baking sheet. Place another sheet of parchment paper on top of the rolled dough on the baking sheet. Roll out the remaining pieces of dough, layering them on the baking sheet, each separated by parchment paper sprinkled with 1 tablespoon of cornmeal. This is an easy way to store the dough as it rests. Wrap the baking sheet in plastic and refrigerate for at least 4 hours, or up to overnight.

Preheat the oven to 350°F.

❯ ❯ ❯

CRICK CRACKS

To make the topping, combine the sesame and nigella seeds.

Transfer one sheet of dough to a baking sheet. Leave the others in the refrigerator.

Using a dough docker or a fork, prick holes over the surface of the dough to prevent the dough from bubbling up as it bakes. Brush the dough with water. Sprinkle with ¼ teaspoon of salt and one-quarter of the seed mixture. Using a ruler and a pizza cutter or a knife, cut the dough into 3-inch squares. It is okay to leave odd pieces on the edges to nibble after they are baked rather than making a perfect shape. The dough will get tough if rerolled.

Bake, rotating the pan, until lightly browned, 8 to 10 minutes. Watch the first pan for exact timing. Continue baking the remaining dough. If the oven can hold more than one sheet at a time, keep the remaining two chilled while baking the first two.

Set aside to cool. Store in an airtight container for up to 3 days.

Our Sofra pita is shaped into balls and baked as puffy pillows, which is different from traditional pita. It is surprisingly easy to make. We've also provided instructions for rolling it out to make pita pockets. This same dough is used as a base for Za'atar Bread (page 114) and Spicy Lamb Pide (page 141). ◆ **MAURA**

MAKES 10 PITAS

PITA BREAD

1¼ cups warm water, plus more as needed

2¼ teaspoons active dry yeast

2 tablespoons honey

3 cups all-purpose flour

1½ teaspoons kosher salt

2 tablespoons extra-virgin olive oil

Combine the water, yeast, and honey in the bowl of a stand mixer. Whisk by hand to combine. Set aside until foamy, 5 minutes.

Add the flour, salt, and olive oil. Using the dough hook, knead on low speed until a smooth dough is formed, 5 minutes.

Remove the dough from the bowl and, using your hands, knead into a smooth ball. Place in a clean, lightly oiled bowl; cover with plastic wrap and let rise at room temperature until doubled in size, about 1 hour.

Lightly flour a work surface. Put the dough on the work surface and form into a rectangle. Cut into 10 equal pieces. Form each into a ball and roll on a clean work surface by cupping your hand around the dough and rolling in a circular motion. Repeat with the remaining dough. Place the dough balls back on the prepared work surface. Cover with plastic wrap and let rise at room temperature for 1 hour.

Preheat the oven to 400°F. Line a baking sheet with parchment paper.

Place the balls of dough on the prepared baking sheet, 2 inches apart. Bake until light golden brown.

Store pita in an airtight container or a zip-top bag. Pita is best served the same day but will keep 3 days.

VARIATION For pita pockets, use a rolling pin to roll each ball into a 6-inch circle. Place on a prepared baking sheet; you can probably fit three or four at once. Bake at 400°F until they puff up and are lightly browned, about 5 minutes. Let cool on the sheet.

Cassie Piuma, the chef at Sarma, our sister restaurant, wanted a cracker that tasted like a falafel to accompany one of her meze. After a few attempts, I decided to work with a tried-and-true recipe, our Crick Cracks (page 67). By adding some chickpea flour, tahini, and the spices in Ana's falafel—cumin and allspice—we had the perfect crisp cracker for her dip. This is a brilliant cracker, and a perfect example of how our teams at Oleana, Sarma, and Sofra inspire each other. ◆ **MAURA**

MAKES 1 POUND OF CRACKERS, TO SERVE WITH MEZE

FALAFEL CRACKERS

¾ cup buttermilk

2 tablespoons tahini (see page 242)

1½ cups all-purpose flour, plus more for rolling out the dough

½ cup chickpea flour (see note, page 71)

1 tablespoon sugar

2 teaspoons kosher salt

1 tablespoon ground cumin

¼ teaspoon ground allspice

1 stick (4 ounces) unsalted butter, chilled and cut into ¼-inch cubes

4 tablespoons cornmeal

2 tablespoons sesame seeds

Combine the buttermilk and tahini in a small bowl and set aside.

Combine the flours, sugar, 1 teaspoon of the salt, cumin, allspice, and butter in the bowl of a stand mixer fitted with a paddle attachment. Mix on low speed until the butter is in very small, almost invisible pieces. Add the buttermilk mixture all at once and mix until it is incorporated and forms a wet dough.

Lightly flour a work surface. Transfer the dough to the floured surface and press into an 8 by 4-inch rectangle. Wrap in plastic and refrigerate overnight.

Lightly flour a work surface. Divide the dough into quarters. Line a baking sheet with parchment paper. Work with one piece of dough at a time and keep the other portions of dough in the refrigerator. Roll each into a rectangle approximately 12 inches by 13 inches and about ¹⁄₁₆ inch thick. It is more important that the dough be rolled to ¹⁄₁₆ inch thickness than it be a perfect rectangle.

Sprinkle the parchment paper with 1 tablespoon cornmeal. Pick up the rolled sheet of dough and place on the prepared pan. Place another sheet of parchment paper on top. Sprinkle with 1 tablespoon cornmeal and roll out the remaining three pieces of dough, layering them and separating them with parchment paper. This is an easy, space-saving way to store the dough in the refrigerator as it rests. Wrap the baking sheet with plastic wrap and refrigerate for 4 hours, or up to overnight.

Preheat the oven to 350°F.

CHICKPEA FLOUR Also known as garbanzo bean flour or gram flour, chickpea flour is naturally gluten-free, made from ground chickpeas. It is available from Bob's Red Mill online and at health food stores.

Place one sheet of dough onto the baking sheet, still on its parchment paper. Dock the dough using a dough docker or by pricking it all over with a fork. This will prevent the dough from bubbling up when it's baking. Brush the dough lightly with water. Sprinkle with ¼ teaspoon salt and one-quarter of the sesame seeds over the sheet. Using a ruler and a pizza cutter or knife, cut into 3-inch squares. It is okay to have odd pieces around the edges to nibble on.

Bake for 6 minutes, then rotate the pan and bake for an additional 6 to 7 minutes, until lightly browned. Repeat with the remaining sheets of dough. If you have space in the oven, you can bake two pans at the same time.

Set aside to cool in the pan. These will keep stored in an airtight container for 3 days.

Fattoush is a classic Middle Eastern salad made with chopped tomato, romaine, herbs, and cucumber. It's usually topped with small pieces of crispy, deep-fried pita bread and generously sprinkled with sumac, a delicious, tart spice with a slight raisin or sun-dried quality and bright crimson color. It's what makes fattoush taste so lemony. In the fall, early winter, or spring, when apples and radishes are looking good, this salad has incredible, bright flavors that pop in the mouth. In the wintertime, I like to substitute escarole for the romaine, pomegranates for the apples, and mandarins for the radishes. ◆ **ANA**

SERVES 4 TO 6

GREEN APPLE FATTOUSH

2½ cups pita cut into ½-inch squares (approximately two 6-inch pitas)

10 tablespoons extra-virgin olive oil

1 teaspoon kosher salt

1 head romaine lettuce, outer bruised leaves removed

2 tablespoons pomegranate molasses (see page 240)

1 tablespoon freshly squeezed lemon juice

1 cup coarsely chopped fresh spearmint leaves

1 cup coarsely chopped fresh flat-leaf parsley leaves

2 Persian cucumbers or ½ English cucumber, split in half, seeded and diced small (about 1 cup)

1 cup chopped green apple, core removed

6 radishes or turnips, cubed or thinly sliced

Freshly ground black pepper

2 teaspoons sumac

Preheat the oven to 375°F.

Place the pita squares in a large mixing bowl and coat them with 6 tablespoons of the olive oil, using your hands to almost knead the oil into them. The olive oil must saturate the pita so that they crisp in the oven instead of toast. Sprinkle with ½ teaspoon of the salt and spread onto a baking sheet. Toast until they are crisp and golden, about 20 minutes. Set aside to cool.

Cut the core and the top one-third from the head of romaine and trim off any bruised or damaged leaves. Slice the romaine into thin ribbons. Transfer to a large salad bowl.

Make a dressing by whisking together the pomegranate molasses and lemon juice. Whisk in the remaining 4 tablespoons olive oil slowly, to form an emulsion (it's okay if it separates, but it will coat the salad leaves better if it emulsifies). Add the mint, parsley, cucumber, apple, and radishes to the romaine and season with the remaining ½ teaspoon salt and freshly ground black pepper to taste. Toss well to coat everything with dressing.

Sprinkle the salad with sumac and serve immediately.

In this recipe, yellow split peas are whipped with golden turmeric, garlic, lemon, and honey and served warm or at room temperature with our Za'atar Spiced Almonds, as a spread or an accompaniment to fish or vegetables. I eat it just as is with a spoon or top it with a salad of grated radishes, carrots, or blanched sugar snap peas. This dish is a great substitute for hummus and is a great addition to any meze table. But it's also delicious with grilled fish or roasted chicken. ◆ **ANA**

SERVES 8

YELLOW SPLIT PEAS WITH ZA'ATAR SPICED ALMONDS

½ cup plus 2 tablespoons extra-virgin olive oil

2 small white onions, finely chopped (about 1 cup)

1 teaspoon finely chopped garlic

1 teaspoon ground turmeric

2⅓ cups yellow split peas or lentils, picked through for stones

8 cups water

1 bay leaf

1 tablespoon honey

1 teaspoon kosher salt

Freshly ground black pepper

2 tablespoons freshly squeezed lemon juice

¼ cup coarsely chopped fresh cilantro leaves

1 cup Za'atar Spiced Almonds (page 229)

Place a wide, deep pot over medium heat and add 2 tablespoons olive oil. Stir in the onions, garlic, and turmeric and sweat until the onions are softened, about 5 minutes.

Rinse the split peas in a colander. Stir them into the onions and add the water and bay leaf. Cook, stirring occasionally, until the peas have absorbed all the liquid and are the consistency of chunky mashed potatoes, 40 to 45 minutes. Stir in the honey and season with salt and pepper. Remove the bay leaf and set aside to cool.

Puree the peas in a food processor fitted with a metal blade, adding the lemon juice and remaining ½ cup olive oil, until the mixture is smooth and creamy.

Serve warm or at room temperature, sprinkled with the cilantro and Za'atar Spiced Almonds; serve pita bread, simit (page 43), or raw vegetables alongside. Store covered in the refrigerator up to 4 days.

This lentil salad tastes best when served cold because the flavors need to mingle and mellow. It's a staple on our meze bar in the fall, when dark leafy greens like chard, kale, and collards are at their peak and their sweetest. Remove the stalks if they are large and fibrous looking, but if the chard is young and tender, the stalks are delicious chopped and added to the sauté pan with the onion. ◆ **ANA**

SERVES 4 TO 6

SYRIAN-STYLE LENTILS WITH CHARD

1½ cups brown or French green lentils (lentilles du Puy), picked through for stones

3 teaspoons kosher salt, plus more to taste

½ cup extra-virgin olive oil

1½ cups sliced sweet onion, such as Ailsa Craig, Vidalia, or Walla Walla

1 tablespoon finely chopped garlic

10 chard leaves, stalks removed, sliced into thin ribbons (about 3 cups)

1 tablespoon freshly squeezed lemon juice

2 tablespoons grape molasses (pekmez, see page 233) or pomegranate molasses (see page 240)

¾ cup chopped fresh cilantro leaves (about 1 bunch)

Freshly ground black pepper

In a saucepan, bring 6 cups water to a boil over high heat. Add the lentils, lower the heat, and simmer until just tender, about 20 minutes. Add 2 teaspoons of the salt and let the lentils stand off the heat for 5 minutes to absorb the salt. If the lentils cool down before they have time to absorb the salt, they will be salty on the outside and not seasoned throughout. Drain and spread them onto a baking sheet to cool.

Meanwhile, place a sauté pan over medium heat and add 2 table-spoons of the olive oil. Add the onion and sauté on low heat until the onion starts to brown, about 10 minutes. Stir in the garlic and chard leaves and cook until the chard wilts and is tender, about 3 minutes.

Combine the lentils in a large mixing bowl with the onion and chard mixture. Add the lemon juice, grape molasses, and remaining 6 tablespoons of olive oil. Add the cilantro and season with the remaining 1 teaspoon salt and the pepper to taste.

Serve at room temperature or chilled. Store covered in the refrigerator for up to 4 days.

COOK'S NOTE Grape or pomegranate molasses is used in place of vinegar to bring bright acidity and tartness to this meze. Both molasses are made from sour fruit juice that is reduced with a little bit of salt to form a concentrated syrup that looks similar to aged balsamic vinegar. Combined with a little lemon juice and olive oil, it makes a delicious dressing.

Although the chickpeas are the stars of this recipe, the most essential part is the delicious cooking liquid that later soaks into crispy pita bread. Resembling another traditional crisp bread dish called fatteh, this recipe is layered like a chickpea casserole with toasted pita on the bottom and stewed chickpeas and their juices on top. The pita bread absorbs flavor from the chickpeas but also creates a soft texture like a dumpling on the bottom. The top part of the casserole stays crisp after it's baked, resulting in two different textures. It then gets topped with whipped avocado and tahini, fried pine nuts, finely chopped beets, and dill. It's best served warm, but at room temperature, it still tastes delicious. ◆ **ANA**

SERVES 8

BREAD HUMMUS, BEET SALAD, AVOCADO, AND TAHINI

2 golden or candy-striped beets

1 cup dried chickpeas, soaked overnight in 6 cups water

1 teaspoon kosher salt, plus more to taste

2 teaspoons finely chopped garlic

¼ cup freshly squeezed lemon juice

1 cup sliced leek whites or sweet onion, such as Ailsa Craig, Vidalia, or Walla Walla

5 tablespoons extra-virgin olive oil

1 tablespoon water (optional)

1 (12-inch) store-bought pita bread, cut into 1½-inch squares

¼ stick (1 ounce) unsalted butter

2 tablespoons pine nuts

2 large ripe avocados, pitted

¼ cup tahini (see page 242)

2 tablespoons plain whole-milk Greek yogurt

1 teaspoon ground cumin

1 tablespoon chopped fresh dill leaves

Freshly ground black pepper

Cut off the top ends of the beets so that some of the beet is exposed and cover them with cold water in a saucepan. Bring to a boil over high heat and then lower the heat to medium-low. Cook uncovered until tender when pierced with a knife, 30 to 40 minutes. If the water evaporates, add more water to keep the beets covered while cooking. Drain and set aside to cool. When the beets are cool enough to handle, use a paper towel to help rub off the skin.

Drain the chickpeas and place them in a large saucepan with 6 cups water. Bring to a boil over high heat and then lower the heat to medium-low and simmer until they are tender, about 40 minutes, using a ladle to skim off any foam that rises to the top. Off the heat, add 1 teaspoon salt to the water and allow the chickpeas to absorb the salt for 10 minutes. Stir in 1 teaspoon of the garlic and 1 tablespoon of the lemon juice. Keep warm or set aside.

Preheat the oven to 350°F.

Meanwhile, in a sauté pan, sweat the leeks with 1 tablespoon of the olive oil and 1 tablespoon water over medium-low heat until they are very soft and tender, about 5 minutes. Don't let them get brown or they will be bitter. If you are using onions, you don't need to add water and it's okay to lightly brown or caramelize them. Season with salt to taste.

Combine the bread and 3 tablespoons of the olive oil in a large mixing bowl and, using your hands, rub the oil into the bread. Transfer to a baking sheet and bake until golden and crisp, about 8 minutes.

❯ ❯ ❯

▶ ▶ ▶ BREAD HUMMUS, BEET SALAD, AVOCADO, AND TAHINI

In a small skillet over medium heat, melt the butter. Add the pine nuts and cook, stirring, until golden but not brown, about 3 minutes. Season with salt to taste and set aside the pan.

Scoop the avocados into a food processor and add the tahini, yogurt, cumin, remaining 1 teaspoon of garlic, and remaining 3 tablespoons of lemon juice; puree until smooth and creamy. Season with salt to taste.

To assemble the dish, scatter the bread squares on the bottom of a 9½-inch round cast-iron pan, cazuela, or glass pie pan. Reheat the chickpeas in their pan over medium-low heat. Taste the broth and the chickpeas to make sure they are nicely seasoned and add more salt if necessary. Ladle the chickpeas and some of the broth over the bread, making sure the liquid comes only halfway up the bread. The bottom of the bread should be wet but the top should remain crispy. Top the chickpea mixture with the leeks.

Bake until the liquid is absorbed and everything is hot and the top is crispy, about 15 minutes.

Meanwhile, dice the beets and toss them with the remaining 2 table-spoons of olive oil and the dill in a small bowl. Add salt and pepper to taste. Spoon the beets on top of the warm casserole and sprinkle with pine nuts.

Serve the avocado-tahini in a small bowl on the side for topping the hummus.

HUMMUS When you buy hummus at the grocery store, you think you know what good hummus is. And then one day, you visit Lebanon or Israel and you eat real hummus. You realize it's not just a dip for vegetables or crackers. It is a staple as versatile as any, and it can be made to fit your mood and any meal.

Hummus starts with a smooth, creamy base of chickpeas loaded with delicious olive oil, garlic, and tahini, which then gets whipped and spooned into a shallow bowl (called a hummus bowl, of course), where a well is formed in the center to hold extra olive oil and different toppings, such as ground lamb and pine nuts or stewed chickpeas with garlicky juices and parsley.

Hummus means "chickpeas" in Arabic, so as far as I'm concerned, if the centerpiece of the dish is chickpeas, you can call it hummus. A fun fact to remember is that when chickpeas are combined with tahini, a complete protein is formed, and it becomes a meal. The advantage to making hummus yourself is that you can control the quality and quantity of both the olive oil and the tahini.

We've included here a few of our favorite variations on hummus that we think you will want to make over and over. We hope these recipes inspire you to consider hummus as a blank canvas for many different toppings and prove that hummus is not just a dip for vegetables. When you embellish it, you have an incredible and balanced meal.

My friend Ayfer Unsal is from Gaziantep in the southeastern part of Turkey. In 1998, she invited me to come and study the food of her hometown, where I tasted things like walnuts with tomatoes and pomegranate molasses! I've never been the same since. In 2012, I took a group of customers to retrace the steps of my first visit to Turkey with Ayfer and I rummaged through an old notebook to find some dishes that we had cooked together. I found something that resembled the following recipe and have re-created this summer tomato dish inspired by those original notes and lessons from Ayfer. The rich, warm combination of walnuts, tart pomegranate molasses, and tomatoes will always remind me of my first visit to Turkey. I love the touch of sweet cinnamon that hides in this blend of flavors. ◆ **ANA**

SERVES 4

TOMATO, WALNUT, AND POMEGRANATE SALAD

3 cups ripe cherry tomatoes or Sungold tomatoes, split in half or in quarters if large

½ teaspoon kosher salt, plus more to taste

2 tablespoons pomegranate molasses (see page 240)

1 teaspoon freshly squeezed lemon juice

¼ teaspoon ground cinnamon

¼ cup extra-virgin olive oil

Freshly ground black pepper

1 cup walnuts, lightly toasted and finely chopped

¼ cup chopped fresh flat-leaf parsley leaves

2 tablespoons chopped fresh spearmint leaves

Lightly season the tomatoes with the salt and let them sit in a colander over a large mixing bowl for 10 minutes to drain off any juices, catching the juices in the bowl.

Whisk the tomato juices, pomegranate molasses, lemon juice, cinnamon, and olive oil in a small bowl. Season with salt and pepper to taste.

Add the tomatoes, walnuts, parsley, and mint to the dressing and mix well. Season with more salt to taste and serve right away.

This version of hummus has no tahini in it and is inspired by a dish that I was served in Cappadocia, a region in central Turkey where hummus is made with half butter and half olive oil and served warm—usually with tomato, olives, and paper-thin slices of basturma, a cured spiced beef. In Lebanon, it is common to see classic tavern-style hummus topped with browned lamb and pine nuts and served at room temperature. My recipe combines the two traditions into a version of hummus that could be served alone, as a meal. The very creamy chickpea base is spooned into a shallow bowl, where you create a well that acts as a pocket to collect the lamb and its juices, along with butter and chiles. ◆ **ANA**

SERVES 4 TO 6

WARM BUTTERED HUMMUS, SPICY LAMB, AND PINE NUTS

1 cup dried chickpeas, soaked overnight in 6 cups water

1 bay leaf

Pinch of baking soda

1¾ teaspoons kosher salt, plus more to taste

3 tablespoons unsalted butter

3 tablespoons extra-virgin olive oil

1 tablespoon freshly squeezed lemon juice

¾ teaspoon ground cumin

8 ounces ground lamb

⅛ teaspoon ground allspice

¼ teaspoon freshly ground black pepper

1 large ripe tomato, or ½ cup canned tomato

4 green onions, mostly the white part, finely chopped

1½ teaspoons harissa, or 1 teaspoon Maras pepper (see page 236)

1 tablespoon finely chopped fresh flat-leaf parsley leaves

2 tablespoons pine nuts

Drain the chickpeas and combine them in a large saucepan with 6 cups fresh water. Add the bay leaf and baking soda and bring to a boil over high heat. Lower the heat to medium-low and simmer until the chickpeas are tender and almost falling apart, about 45 minutes, using a ladle to skim any foam that rises to the surface. Add 1 teaspoon salt, stir, and set aside for 5 minutes to absorb the salt. Reserve ¾ cup of the cooking liquid and drain in a colander. Remove the bay leaf.

While the chickpeas are still hot, process them in a food processor fitted with a metal blade until they are finely ground and start to resemble cookie dough. The chickpeas will form a ball in the machine as they become smooth enough. Add 2 tablespoons of the butter and 2 tablespoons of the olive oil in a slow, steady stream. Next slowly add the lemon juice, the cumin, and half of the chickpea cooking liquid and continue to blend until very, very smooth and creamy. Add 1 to 2 tablespoons more of the cooking liquid if it seems too thick. The consistency should be creamy, like mayonnaise. Season with salt to taste.

Meanwhile, in a large sauté pan over medium-high heat, heat the remaining 1 tablespoon olive oil and brown the lamb, seasoning with ½ teaspoon salt. Break the lamb up so that it crumbles as it browns. Continue to cook until the bits of lamb are golden brown and cooked through, about 6 minutes. Add the allspice, black pepper, tomato, and any remaining chickpea cooking liquid and continue to cook until half the liquid is absorbed, about 4 minutes.

Stir in the green onions and harissa and simmer until the mixture is thick and juicy and most of the liquid has been absorbed, about 3 minutes. Remove from the heat and stir in the chopped parsley.

Meanwhile, melt the remaining 1 tablespoon butter in a small skillet over medium-low heat. Add the pine nuts and fry until golden brown, about 4 minutes. Season with the remaining ¼ teaspoon salt.

To serve, scrape the hummus into the center of a large shallow serving bowl, forming a large mound in the center of the bowl. Use the back of a large serving spoon and, starting from the center, smooth it around towards the edges of the shallow bowl. As you smooth the hummus, create a lip on the outer edge to catch the lamb. Try to form a large, shallow ½-inch-deep well in the center to hold the lamb juices.

Spoon the lamb into the well, distributing it evenly all the way towards the edges. Sprinkle the top with the buttery pine nuts and serve warm.

COOK'S NOTES You can prepare this platter ahead of time and cover it with foil. When you are ready to serve it, warm it in a 300°F oven for 15 minutes.

To make smooth, creamy hummus, add a pinch of baking soda to the water while you are cooking the chickpeas. This will help soften their skins quickly. Puree the chickpeas first with garlic and salt in a food processor, for about 3 minutes. When the chickpeas are finely ground and almost resemble cookie dough (it starts to form a ball in the food processor), add the lemon, tahini, and olive oil slowly with the motor running, seasoning everything with cumin and salt. Continue to blend for 5 to 8 minutes longer, until it's as smooth as possible.

I love to eat this variation of hummus in the fall with grated radishes or pomegranate seeds sprinkled over top. There is something extremely decadent about serving the warm walnuts in the center of this hummus. You'll want to do it every single time. ◆ **ANA**

SERVES 4

WALNUT HUMMUS, POMEGRANATE, AND CILANTRO

1 cup dried chickpeas, soaked overnight in 6 cups water

Pinch of baking soda

1 teaspoon kosher salt, plus more to taste

2 cloves garlic, peeled

1 teaspoon ground cumin

3 tablespoons freshly squeezed lemon juice

6 tablespoons tahini (see page 242)

2 tablespoons extra-virgin olive oil

¼ cup walnut oil

½ cup coarsely chopped walnuts

1 tablespoon unsalted butter or extra-virgin olive oil

1 teaspoon Maras pepper (see page 236)

¼ cup pomegranate seeds

¼ cup coarsely chopped fresh cilantro leaves

Drain the chickpeas and combine them in a large saucepan with 6 cups fresh water. Add the baking soda and bring to a boil over high heat. Lower the heat to medium-low and simmer until tender and almost falling apart, about 45 minutes, using a ladle to skim any foam that rises to the surface. Add 1 teaspoon salt, stir, and set aside for 5 minutes to absorb the salt. Reserve ½ cup of the cooking liquid and drain in a colander.

Preheat the oven to 350°F.

Put the garlic in a food processor fitted with a metal blade and process until finely chopped. Add the chickpeas and blend until finely ground and starting to resemble cookie dough. The chickpeas will form a ball in the machine as they become smooth enough. Add the cumin, lemon juice, and half of the chickpea cooking liquid and process. Add the tahini and oils slowly in a smooth stream as the machine is running, stopping once to scrape the sides of the bowl. Add 1 to 2 tablespoons more of the cooking liquid if it seems too thick. The consistency should be creamy, like mayonnaise. Season with sale to taste.

Put the walnuts on a baking sheet. Melt the butter in a small saucepan and pour it over the walnuts. Toss the walnuts to coat them evenly with the butter and roast until they are lightly toasted, about 7 minutes. Sprinkle with Maras pepper and lightly season with salt to taste.

To serve, scrape the hummus into the center of a large shallow serving bowl, forming a large mound in the center of the bowl. Use the back of a large serving spoon and, starting from the center, smooth it around towards the edges of the bowl. As you smooth the hummus, create a lip on the outer edge. Try to form a large, shallow ½-inch deep well in the center to hold the walnuts. Sprinkle the pomegranate seeds and cilantro evenly over the center. If the walnuts have cooled, warm them again in the oven for 4 minutes and evenly distribute them in the center over the pomegranate and cilantro. Serve immediately.

Buttermilk, like lemon juice, brings acidity to a rich hummus, but it also blends into a beautiful blond-colored puree with a light and creamy texture. It makes a delicious pairing with fall vegetables like celery root or watermelon radishes that are dressed with buttermilk and mustard, which mimics French celery root remoulade or Turkish celery root salad with yogurt dressing. I always love something crunchy on my hummus, and it's usually a nut or a rich seed like the Mexican pumpkin seed, or pepita. Pepitas get very plump and crisp when they are roasted and don't have the chewiness that larger pumpkin seeds have. ◆ **ANA**

SERVES 4

BUTTERMILK HUMMUS WITH CELERY ROOT AND PUMPKIN SEEDS

1 cup dried chickpeas, soaked overnight in 6 cups water

Pinch of baking soda

1 teaspoon kosher salt, plus more to taste

2 cloves garlic, peeled

¾ teaspoon sweet Hungarian paprika

½ teaspoon ground cumin

1 tablespoon plus 1 teaspoon freshly squeezed lemon juice

2 tablespoons tahini (see page 242)

3 tablespoons extra-virgin olive oil

5 to 6 tablespoons buttermilk or plain whole-milk Greek yogurt

½ medium-sized celery root or 2 watermelon radishes

2 teaspoons Dijon mustard

1 tablespoon mayonnaise

2 green onions, mostly the white part, finely chopped

Freshly ground black pepper

¼ cup roasted pepitas

2 tablespoons coarsely chopped fresh cilantro leaves

2 large basil leaves, torn into bite-size strips

Drain the chickpeas and combine them in a large saucepan with 6 cups fresh water. Add the baking soda and bring to a boil over high heat. Lower the heat to medium-low and simmer until tender and almost falling apart, about 45 minutes, using a ladle to skim any foam that rises to the surface. Add 1 teaspoon salt, stir, and set aside for 5 minutes to absorb the salt. Drain in a colander.

Put the garlic in a food processor fitted with a metal blade and process until finely chopped. Add the chickpeas and blend until finely ground and starting to resemble cookie dough. The chickpeas will form a ball in the machine as they become smooth enough. Add ½ teaspoon of the paprika, the cumin, and 1 tablespoon of the lemon juice and process until smooth. With the machine running, add the tahini, 1 tablespoon of the olive oil, and 4 tablespoons of the buttermilk, stopping once to scrape the sides of the bowl. Add 1 tablespoon more of the buttermilk if it seems too thick. Season with salt to taste.

Peel the celery root by first cutting off both of the ends so that it can stand upright on the cutting board. Using a knife, follow the shape of the celery root, starting at the top and working your way down to the bottom, trying to take off just the thick skin. If you have a very sharp peeler, you can use it, but often the skin is too thick and needs to be removed with a knife. Try to keep the celery root dry because it will brown if it gets wet. Cut the celery root in half and reserve the other half for another use. Using a mandoline or a knife, slice the celery root as thinly as possible. Stack the slices on top of each other and julienne them into ⅛-inch matchsticks.

In a large mixing bowl, combine the Dijon mustard with the remaining 1 teaspoon lemon juice and whisk until smooth. Add the remaining 1 tablespoon buttermilk and 1 tablespoon of the olive oil. Whisk until smooth and emulsified. Add the mayonnaise and whisk until smooth again. Season with salt to taste.

Add the celery root and green onions to the dressing in the mixing bowl. Using your hands, knead the dressing into the celery root until every piece is nicely coated with dressing. Season with salt and pepper to taste.

To serve, scrape the hummus into the center of a large shallow serving bowl, forming a large mound in the center of the bowl. Use the back of a large serving spoon and, starting from the center, smooth it around towards the edges of the bowl. As you smooth the hummus, create a lip on the outer edge. Try to form a large shallow ½-inch-deep well in the center to hold the celery root. Mound the celery root in the center of the well and sprinkle the pepitas, cilantro, and basil over the top. Just before serving, dust the edges of the hummus with the remaining ¼ teaspoon paprika and drizzle the whole platter with the remaining 1 tablespoon olive oil.

FLATBREADS

In the Middle East, flatbread is used like a sponge to absorb the juices of chopped vegetables and roasted meats as they rest or cook. Ana is always overcome by the urge to fight over the highly seasoned bread after a kebab has rested on it for a few minutes. Many times she has been to Durumzade, a small durum (Turkish for "wrap") stand in Istanbul, where each time she is mesmerized by the way the chef uses the bread to pat the meat while it's roasting on a skewer, to absorb juices that might otherwise bead up and roll into the fire. The bread catches any escaping flavor and is so carefully folded and layered as it's assembled that the result is a perfect ratio of flavored bread, vegetables, meat, and pickles.

The flatbreads in this chapter all have a similar purpose. There are a variety of fillings that must not be spread on too thick or the sandwich becomes heavy or soggy. These breads are neither overstuffed nor oozing with melted cheese. As you assemble them, it's important to remember each is a careful balance. They are great accompaniments to meze or delicious on their own.

The variety of breads, and fillings, is endless. Before Sofra opened, Ana was gifted a copy of Barbara Massoud's *Man'oushe*, a beautiful book that inspired the experience and purpose of Sofra. Man'oushe, or manoushe, a common street food in Lebanon, is a yeasted flatbread spread with a choice of different fillings, then folded over for easy eating. Massoud's images of these perfect little sandwiches were a part of our vision board as Sofra was conceived. The most common manoushe is bathed in olive oil mixed with za'atar.

In Turkey, gozleme, also a common street food, is made from a nonyeasted dough called yufka, similar to a very stretchy tortilla. This is the dough we use at Sofra to make all of our flatbreads, as it is thinner and easier to roll out then many of the alternatives.

In the farmers' market in Turkey, you might see a woman sitting on the ground, rolling out very thin, large rounds of this dough using a skinny rolling pin. She drops a pile of chopped spinach on the dough and spreads it out over half. Using her fingers, she breaks small chunks of feta cheese over the top of the spinach and then pours on some olive oil. The large hotplate sizzles next to her. It is round and convex, like an upside-down wok. She folds the gozleme in half and drapes it over the hotplate, and the aroma of cooking bread wafts up. Folding, turning, and flipping, she traps the fillings inside the pancake and cooks both sides until they are lightly toasted. It doesn't take long.

Another popular filling is shawarma, or marinated lamb, beef, or chicken that has been roasted until the edges caramelize. It is shaved and served on bread. The shawarma, or doner in Turkey, is shaved off the skewer one sandwich at a time, to fall into a glove of pita bread. It is then topped with sauce and chopped vegetables and/or pickles before it is rolled up.

It was difficult but we managed to put a selection of our most beloved flatbreads in one chapter. But feel free to experiment to find your own favorite flavors!

Yufka is nonleavened dough that is thinner than a tortilla and heartier than phyllo dough; it has a substantial bite but is still very flaky. It is rumored to be the original form of phyllo. Yufka is used to make many flatbreads, pastries, and borek, a baked or fried pie found in Turkey and the Middle East. ◆ **MAURA**

MAKES 6 YUFKA

YUFKA DOUGH

1⅔ cups all-purpose flour, plus more for dusting

1 teaspoon kosher salt

⅔ cup warm water

2 tablespoons extra-virgin olive oil, plus a little more as needed

In a medium bowl, whisk together the flour and salt. Make a well in the center and pour in the water and olive oil. Using your fingers, draw the flour in from all sides, working the mixture until it's sticky and forms into a ball. Turn the dough onto a floured surface and knead until smooth and elastic, about 3 minutes. Transfer back to the bowl, drizzle with a little bit of oil, and turn to coat. Cover with plastic wrap and let rest at room temperature for at least 4 hours, or up to overnight.

Divide the dough in half, then divide each half into three equal pieces; you should have six equal pieces, each weighing about 2 ounces.

Roll out each yufka ball into a very thin 8- to 9-inch round, using plenty of flour to keep the dough from sticking to the rolling pin. Stack them on top of each other with a piece of parchment paper between them and plenty of flour or lay them out slightly overlapping on a baking sheet.

Heat an 11- to 12-inch cast-iron skillet or nonstick pan over medium heat and cook the yufka on one side until it starts to bubble up and lightly brown on the bottom, about 2 minutes. You only need to partially cook each flatbread at this stage; don't get them too crispy or they will be dry and hard to work with. Stack them on top of each other as you cook each one so that they lightly steam and keep each other soft and pliable.

If you are not using immediately, transfer the warm yufka to a large zip-top plastic bag and store at room temperature up to overnight. You can also freeze the yufka for up to 2 weeks. After thawing, reheat briefly in a skillet over medium heat before using.

COOK'S NOTE When making flatbreads that require yufka dough, you can substitute commercial yufka, country-style phyllo, or lavash bread, but the results won't be as flaky and tender as the yufka you make from scratch. All of the above substitutes are precooked so you can fill them and toast them as described in each recipe.

Inspired by the gozleme sellers at the farmers' markets in Turkey, I developed this flatbread. It is stuffed with a mixture of three different cheeses that mimic a fetalike white cheese called, naturally, Turkish white cheese. It's sprinkled with a handful of chopped spinach and my favorite combination of fresh herbs: parsley, mint, and dill. ◆ **ANA**

MAKES 6 LARGE FLATBREADS; SERVES 6 TO 12

SPINACH AND THREE CHEESE GOZLEME

Yufka Dough (page 95)

1 tablespoon extra-virgin olive oil

1 cup finely chopped Spanish onion

1 cup ricotta cheese

¾ cup crumbled feta cheese, preferably sheep's or goat's milk

1 cup grated kasseri cheese (see page 236)

½ teaspoon kosher salt, plus more as needed

¼ cup chopped fresh flat-leaf parsley leaves

¼ cup chopped fresh spearmint leaves

¼ cup chopped fresh dill leaves

Freshly ground black pepper

4½ cups spinach, cut into thin ribbons

Follow the directions to make the yufka dough, transfer to a zip-top plastic bag, and store at room temperature.

Heat the olive oil and onion in a sauté pan over medium-low heat and sweat the onion until softened, about 8 minutes. Using a spatula, scrape into a large mixing bowl and add the ricotta cheese, feta cheese, kasseri cheese, salt, parsley, mint, dill, and pepper to taste.

When you are ready to assemble, put about ⅓ cup cheese filling on each yufka and smooth it to the edges in a very thin layer. Sprinkle evenly with ¾ cup spinach and season lightly with salt. Fold the left side in towards the middle and then the right side towards the middle, overlapping by about ½ inch, to form a rectangle shape with an open top and bottom.

When the gozleme are assembled, heat an 11- to 12-inch cast-iron or nonstick pan over medium-low heat. Place two gozleme at a time, seam side down, in the pan. Cook until the filling is hot, the spinach is wilted, and the bread is lightly toasted on one side but still soft on the other, 3 to 4 minutes. Flip to the other side and cook 1 minute more to heat through. Place on a tray and cover with aluminum foil to keep warm while you cook the remaining four gozleme. Cut into halves or strips and serve immediately.

Aida Sarkis, the mother of my friend Hashim Sarkis, gave this recipe to me. Aida now lives in Beirut but is from Moukhtara in the Chouf region of Lebanon, where this recipe is from. I've fallen in love with the rich, nutty, tart flavors of the filling and have used it (leaving out the zucchini) to stuff squash and even as a crust for fish before being baked. Though manoushe is traditionally made with yeasted dough, my yufka recipe works wonderfully and is easier to roll out to the ideal thinness for showcasing the filling. ◆ **ANA**

MAKES 6 LARGE FLATBREADS; SERVES 6 TO 12

SESAME-WALNUT MANOUSHE WITH ZUCCHINI

Yufka Dough (page 95)

2 cups grated zucchini or cousa squash

½ teaspoon kosher salt

1 Spanish onion

2 tablespoons plus 2 teaspoons extra-virgin olive oil

¼ cup walnuts, lightly toasted and finely ground in a food processor

½ cup grated haloumi cheese

3 to 4 ounces crumbled feta, or 4 ounces buffalo milk mozzarella, broken up into small pieces

1 tablespoon pomegranate molasses (see page 240)

¾ teaspoon Maras pepper (see page 236)

2 tablespoons toasted sesame seeds (see page 241)

2 tablespoons chopped fresh flat-leaf parsley leaves

¼ cup sliced fresh basil leaves

Follow the directions to make the yufka dough, transfer to a zip-top plastic bag, and store at room temperature.

Sprinkle the zucchini with the salt and let stand in a colander or a bowl for 5 minutes to draw out the water.

Using the large holes of a box grater, grate the onion over a plate with sides. Place in a strainer and rinse with cold water. Squeeze dry by placing it in the palm of your hand, making a ball and then flattening it as hard as you can to get the water out. Repeat the squeezing with the zucchini.

Sweat the zucchini with 2 teaspoons olive oil in a small sauté pan over medium heat until it is barely tender, about 3 minutes.

In a large mixing bowl, combine the onion, zucchini, walnuts, haloumi, feta, pomegranate molasses, Maras pepper, sesame seeds, remaining 2 tablespoons olive oil, parsley, and basil. Mix until the filling is spreadable.

When you are ready to assemble, put about ⅓ cup filling on each yufka and smooth it to the edges in a very thin layer. Fold the left side in towards the middle and then the right side towards the middle, overlapping by about ½ inch, to form a rectangle shape with an open top and bottom.

When the manoushe are assembled, heat an 11- to 12-inch cast-iron or nonstick pan over medium-low heat. Place two manoushe at a time, seam side down, in the pan. Cook until the filling is hot and the bread is lightly toasted on one side but still soft on the other, 3 to 4 minutes. Flip to the other side and cook 1 minute more to heat through. Place on a tray and cover with aluminum foil to keep warm while you cook the remaining four manoushe. Cut into halves or strips and serve immediately.

The combination of cumin and orange creates a flavor that is unmistakably Greek. Pickled peppers and orange zest cut through the richness of this interpretation of loukanika, a popular Greek-style sausage. This flatbread is a Sofra favorite and has been on our menu since the day we opened. In Greece, this pita would be made with a yeasted flatbread like the manoushe but I find my yufka recipe easier to work with to achieve a thinness that's proportionate to the filling. You can substitute a store-bought pita for this that is already cooked. You will want to split the pita in half (or butterfly it) so that you have two rounds to work with and so that it remains thin. The method is the same as for gozleme but the flavors are something you would taste only in Greece. ◆ **ANA**

MAKES 6 LARGE FLATBREADS; SERVES 6 TO 12

SAUSAGE PITA WITH CUMIN, ORANGE, AND OLIVE

1 teaspoon grapeseed oil

1 pound ground pork

¼ teaspoon ground allspice

¼ teaspoon Maras pepper (see page 236)

1 teaspoon dried oregano

1½ teaspoons ground cumin

1½ teaspoons sweet Hungarian paprika

½ teaspoon sugar

1¼ teaspoons kosher salt

¼ teaspoon freshly ground black pepper

Grated zest of 1 orange

2 tablespoons chopped fresh flat-leaf parsley leaves

12 ounces crumbled feta cheese

½ stick (2 ounces) unsalted butter, at room temperature

Yufka Dough (page 95)

6 to 8 pickled pepperoncini, stemmed and coarsely chopped

½ cup pitted green olives, such as Lucques or Picholine, coarsely chopped

In a 10-inch sauté pan, heat the grapeseed oil over medium-high heat until hot. Add the pork, breaking it up, until it turns golden on one side, about 2 minutes. Add the allspice, Maras pepper, oregano, cumin, paprika, sugar, salt, and pepper and mix in the spices as you continue to stir and break up the meat. When the meat is cooked through, about 4 minutes, stir in the orange zest and parsley. Drain the sausage in a colander and set aside to cool. If the sausage seems very coarse with large clumps, chop it so that it's a fine crumble.

Meanwhile, in a food processor fitted with a metal blade, blend the feta and butter until very smooth and creamy, like mayonnaise. Set aside until you are ready to assemble.

When you are ready to assemble, put 2 tablespoons feta butter on each yufka and smooth it to the edges in a very thin layer. Sprinkle with about ⅓ cup sausage mixture and distribute it evenly, using the back of a spoon. Sprinkle 1 tablespoon pepperoncini and 1 tablespoon olives over each pita. Fold the left side in towards the middle and then the right side towards the middle, overlapping by about ½ inch, to form a rectangle shape with an open top and bottom.

When the pitas are assembled, heat an 11- to 12-inch cast-iron or nonstick pan over medium-low heat. Place two pitas at a time, seam side down, in the pan. Cook until the filling is hot and the bread is lightly toasted on one side but still soft on the other, 3 to 4 minutes. Flip to the other side and cook for 1 minute more to heat through. Place on a tray and cover with aluminum foil to keep warm while you cook the remaining four pitas. Cut into halves or strips and serve immediately.

My shawarma revelation occurred in a Lebanese deli in an Armenian neighborhood of Los Angeles. I had an hour to kill and popped into a hole in the wall that my Uncle Rik swore made the best shawarma. He was right. It wasn't the meat itself, or the sauce, that made it so incredibly good, but rather, the perfect, restrained balance of the chewy flatbread, the crispy meat, and the punchy sauce. Shawarma isn't typically made at home; street vendors make such delicious versions on giant vertical roasting spits that people go to them for this specialty sandwich. I was determined to create a version for Sofra, using chunks of braised lamb that would achieve a perfectly balanced bite every time. Shawarma are made with pita bread, but the yufka is the perfect thickness and easier to prepare. Store-bought pita works fine if you open up the pocket and use one side per sandwich. ◆ **ANA**

MAKES 6 LARGE FLATBREADS; SERVES 6 TO 12

LAMB SHAWARMA WITH PICKLED CABBAGE AND TAHINI

Yufka Dough (page 95)

4 (10-ounce) bone-in lamb shoulder chops

1 tablespoon grapeseed oil, or more as needed

Kosher salt and freshly ground black pepper

1½ cups dry white wine or water

1 tablespoon ground cumin

4 cloves garlic, smashed and peeled

1 large carrot, cut into 1-inch-thick slices

1 medium-size onion, peeled and cut into 8 wedges

2 tablespoons pomegranate molasses (see page 240)

1½ teaspoons freshly squeezed lemon juice

¼ stick (1 ounce) unsalted butter

Follow the directions to make the yukfa dough, transfer to a zip-top plastic bag, and store at room temperature.

Preheat the oven to 350°F.

Pat the lamb chops dry. Heat the grapeseed oil in a heavy 12-inch skillet over medium-high heat. Working in 2 batches, brown the lamb chops, flipping once, until they are brown on both sides, about 4 minutes total per batch (add more oil for the second batch, if necessary). Season with salt and pepper and transfer to a 9 by 13-inch baking pan.

Pour off any excess fat from the skillet and place it back on the stove over medium-low heat. Add 1 cup of the wine and bring to a simmer, scraping the skillet with a wooden spoon to loosen any browned bits. Pour the wine over the chops. Sprinkle with cumin, then add the garlic, carrot, onion, and remaining ½ cup wine. The liquid should come halfway up the chops; if necessary, add water. Cover the pan with a double thickness of foil and braise in the oven until the meat is fork tender, 1½ hours.

Meanwhile, to make the tahini sauce, in a medium bowl, combine the garlic and lemon juice. Let sit for 5 minutes to soften the garlic flavor, then whisk in the yogurt, tahini, 3 tablespoons olive oil, and salt until smooth. If the sauce is very thick and/or separated, blend it in a food processor, adding another 1 tablespoon olive oil to get it very smooth.

Tahini Sauce

2 cloves garlic, finely chopped

2 tablespoons freshly squeezed lemon juice

½ cup plain whole-milk Greek yogurt

½ cup tahini (see page 242)

3 to 4 tablespoons extra-virgin olive oil

¾ teaspoon kosher salt

Pickled Cabbage

1½ teaspoons extra-virgin olive oil

2 cups thinly sliced red cabbage (about one-quarter of a small cabbage)

½ teaspoon pomegranate molasses (see page 240)

1 tablespoon sherry vinegar, plus more as needed

¼ teaspoon sugar, plus more as needed

Kosher salt and freshly ground black pepper

To make the pickled cabbage, in a 10-inch skillet over medium heat, heat the olive oil. Add the cabbage and cook, stirring occasionally, until just tender, 8 to 10 minutes. Remove from the heat and stir in the pomegranate molasses, vinegar, and sugar. Season with salt, pepper, more vinegar, or sugar to taste.

Transfer the lamb chops to a cutting board and tent loosely with foil to keep warm. Strain the contents of the braising pan through a medium-mesh sieve into a bowl (you should have about 2 cups); discard the solids. Freeze the liquid until the fat rises to the surface, about 15 minutes, then skim it off and discard.

Transfer the liquid to a small saucepan and boil over medium-high heat until it's reduced by half, about 8 minutes. Meanwhile, use your fingers to break the lamb into small chunks, discarding the fat and the bones.

Whisk the pomegranate molasses, lemon juice, and butter into the lamb sauce and stir in the chunks of lamb, gently tossing to coat. Avoid breaking up the chunks too much. Season with salt and pepper to taste.

Divide the lamb mixture among the yufka, spreading it in a strip along one edge to within 1 inch of the sides. Top the lamb with a few tablespoons of the sauce and cabbage and roll up the shawarma tightly, resting them on their seam sides to keep them closed.

Heat a 12-inch cast-iron skillet over medium heat. Working in batches, cook the shawarma, seam side down, until brown and crisped on that side (do not flip), about 3 minutes. Serve immediately.

COOK'S NOTE All the components in the shawarma can be made ahead of time so that it's easy to assemble when needed.

Here is a recipe for an oven-roasted version of this crave-able street food that is usually cooked on a vertical rotisserie. Traditional Lebanese shawarma is topped with a whipped raw garlic sauce, called toum. I prefer a mellower version where the garlic is braised in milk before being whipped with lemon and olive oil. Marinating the chicken in yogurt gives it just the right amount of acid to gently break down the meat's fibers and adds a mild amount of natural sugar for maximum flavor. The careful balance of fragrant spices, just the right amount of garlic, and braising the chicken until the edges are crisp will make it hard to resist eating before it's wrapped in the bread. ◆ **ANA**

MAKES 6 LARGE FLATBREADS; SERVES 6 TO 12

CHICKEN SHAWARMA WITH GARLIC SAUCE AND GREENS

Yufka Dough (page 95)

2 pounds boneless, skinless chicken thighs

1 tablespoon Shawarma Spice (page 220)

1½ teaspoons kosher salt, plus more as needed

½ cup plus 2 tablespoons extra-virgin olive oil

¼ cup plain whole-milk Greek yogurt

3 tablespoons freshly squeezed lemon juice

½ cup peeled garlic cloves

1 cup whole milk

3 cups packed spinach or escarole leaves, cut into thin ribbons

Follow the directions to make the yufka dough, transfer to a zip-top plastic bag, and store at room temperature.

Preheat the oven to 425°F.

In a large glass or stainless steel mixing bowl, combine the chicken thighs with the Shawarma Spice, salt, 2 tablespoons of the olive oil, yogurt, and 2 tablespoons of the lemon juice. Marinate it in the refrigerator for at least 1 hour, or up to 3 hours.

Place the chicken on a heavy baking sheet and add ½ cup water so that the chicken will start cooking with moist heat. Transfer to the oven and roast until the edges are crisp and brown and the chicken is tender when squeezed with a pair of tongs, 40 to 45 minutes. Set aside for 10 minutes. When cool enough to handle, slice it very thinly.

Meanwhile, make the toum. Combine the garlic and milk in a small stainless steel saucepan over low heat. Poach the garlic until it is tender and has absorbed almost all of the milk, about 40 minutes. Put the garlic in the blender with the remaining 1 tablespoon lemon juice and ½ cup olive oil. Blend until smooth and creamy and season with salt to taste.

Divide the chicken mixture among the yufka, spreading it in a strip along one edge to within 1 inch of the sides. Top the chicken with 2 to 3 tablespoons of the sauce and about ½ cup spinach. Roll up the shawarma tightly, resting them on their seam sides to keep them closed.

Heat a 12-inch cast iron skillet over medium heat. Working in batches, cook the shawarma, seam side down, until brown and crisped on that side (do not flip), about 3 minutes. Serve immediately.

This recipe is best made in February through October, the months when butternut squash tastes its best. My husband, farmer Chris, harvests the squash in September, but it takes a month of curing in our greenhouse to sweeten up. Tomato–Brown Butter is one of my favorite condiments because it adds acidity and deep nutty flavors to a simple tomato sauce. Combined with the gusto of sumac, Turkish red pepper flakes, and dried mint, the gozleme is perfectly complete. ◆ **ANA**

MAKES 6 LARGE FLATBREADS; SERVES 6 TO 12

BUTTERNUT SQUASH GOZLEME WITH TOMATO-BROWN BUTTER

Yufka Dough (page 95)

1 cup finely chopped leek, white part only

2 tablespoons extra-virgin olive oil

1½ cups peeled and grated butternut squash (use large holes on a box grater)

¾ cup grated haloumi cheese

1½ teaspoons kosher salt

Freshly ground black pepper

1½ cups Tomato–Brown Butter (page 214)

1 tablespoon sumac (see page 242)

1 tablespoon Maras pepper (see page 236)

1 tablespoon dried spearmint

Follow the directions to make the yufka dough, transfer to a zip-top plastic bag, and store at room temperature.

In a skillet over medium-low heat, sweat the leek in 1 tablespoon olive oil, stirring until it is soft and translucent but not brown, about 5 minutes.

Make the filling by combining the leek, squash, cheese, salt, and pepper to taste in a large mixing bowl.

When you are ready to assemble, put 3 tablespoons Tomato–Brown Butter on each yufka and smooth it to the edges in a very thin layer. You don't want to use as much sauce as you would making a pizza but instead are almost basting the bread with the sauce as if you were spreading it generously with butter. Sprinkle with ⅓ cup squash mixture and distribute it evenly, using the back of a spoon, going all the way to the edges. Sprinkle ½ teaspoon each of sumac, Maras pepper, and mint over each. Fold the left side in towards the middle and then the right side towards the middle, overlapping by about ½ inch, to form a rectangle shape with an open top and bottom.

When the gozleme are assembled, heat an 11- to 12-inch cast-iron or nonstick pan over medium-low heat. Place two gozleme at a time, seam side down, in the pan. Cook until the filling is hot and the bread is lightly toasted on one side but still soft on the other, about 6 minutes. Flip to the other side and cook 1 minute more to heat through. Place them on a tray and cover with aluminum foil to keep warm while you cook the remaining four gozlemes. Cut into halves or strips and serve immediately.

Durum is the Turkish word for "wrap." However, instead of rolling things up like a burrito, there is a careful fold that happens while assembling this sandwich. A good durum is wrap art. The flatbread is basted with spices and marinade first. Typically, grilled or roasted meat is tucked under the first fold. The fold is made from one side of the bread, folding towards the center but stopping at the middle. Then, shredded lettuce, onions with sumac, and chopped tomato are tucked under the second fold. Then the durum is folded in half, resulting in layers of bread and filling throughout each bite. My recipe uses red lentils kneaded with fine bulgur and spices, to make kibbeh or kofte in place of meat. You can add almost any vegetable (such as cabbage, summer squash, and even apple) to this base, just make sure that it's finely chopped. This recipe is my way to elevate the common veggie burrito. ◆ **ANA**

MAKES 6 LARGE FLATBREADS; SERVES 6 TO 12

RED LENTIL DURUM WITH PICKLED PEPPERS

Yufka Dough (page 95)

1 tablespoon unsalted butter

1 small white onion,
finely chopped

½ cup grated carrots, such as
summer squash, or cabbage

2 teaspoons tomato paste

1 teaspoon ground cumin

¾ teaspoon Maras pepper,
plus more to taste (see page 236)

½ cup red lentils

2 cups water

1 teaspoon kosher salt,
plus more to taste

½ cup fine-ground bulgur wheat

2 tablespoons extra-virgin
olive oil

1¼ cups Tomato–Brown Butter
(page 214)

6 to 12 pickled pepperoncini,
stemmed and finely chopped

6 romaine leaves, washed
and cut into thin ribbons
(about 3 cups)

Follow the directions to make the yufka dough, transfer to a zip-top plastic bag, and store at room temperature.

In a medium saucepan over medium-low heat, melt the butter. Add the onion and carrots and sweat, stirring occasionally, until softened, about 5 minutes.

Stir in the tomato paste, cumin, and Maras pepper. Add the lentils and water and bring to a boil over high heat. Lower the heat to medium-low and simmer until the lentils are tender and have absorbed about three-quarters of the liquid, about 10 minutes.

Stir in the salt, bulgur, and olive oil and remove the pan from the heat. Let stand until the liquid is absorbed and the bulgur is softened, about 20 minutes.

Season the lentils with salt to taste. Use a wooden spoon to stir the mixture vigorously, kneading it until it is smooth and not clumpy, about 3 minutes. Transfer to a mixing bowl.

When you are ready to assemble, put 3 tablespoons of the Tomato–Brown Butter on each yufka and smooth it to the edges in a very thin layer (see photos, page 109). You don't want to use as much sauce as you would making a pizza but instead you are almost basting the bread with the sauce as if you were spreading it generously with butter. Scoop ½ cup of the lentil mixture into your hand and make a long rectangular patty. Place it along one edge to within 1 inch of the side.

≫ ≫ ≫

RED LENTIL DURUM WITH PICKLED PEPPERS

Fold one side of the flatbread over it and stop at the middle. Place romaine along the other edge to within 1 inch of the side and sprinkle with about 1 tablespoon pepperoncini. Fold that side over towards the middle so that you have a rectangle with the round ends of the flatbread in the middle. Press down gently with your hand to seal everything and distribute it in an even layer. Then fold the durum in half lengthwise so that you have a long, thin, flat wrap.

When the durum are assembled, heat an 11- to 12-inch cast-iron or nonstick pan over medium-low heat. Place two durum at a time, seam side down, in the pan. Cook until the filling is hot and the bread is lightly toasted on one side but still soft on the other, about 4 minutes. Flip to the other side and cook for 1 minute more to heat through. Place on a tray and cover with aluminum foil to keep warm while you cook the remaining four durum. Cut into halves or strips and serve immediately.

Basturma, or pastirma, from Anatolia, is cured beef with spices like fenugreek, cumin, garlic, and paprika. It is very similar to Italian bresaola and is best sliced thin like most charcuterie. You can find basturma in Greek or Middle Eastern markets. I like using a lot of parsley and fresh oregano in this gozleme to cut through the richness of the spiced beef. ◆ **ANA**

MAKES 6 LARGE FLATBREADS; SERVES 6 TO 12

CABBAGE AND BASTURMA GOZLEME WITH SUMAC ONIONS

Yufka Dough (page 95)

1 tablespoon extra-virgin olive oil

2½ cups shredded arrowhead, Savoy, or green cabbage

Kosher salt and freshly ground black pepper

1 small red onion, thinly sliced

2 teaspoons sumac

¼ cup chopped fresh flat-leaf parsley leaves

2 tablespoons chopped fresh oregano leaves

¾ cup grated kasseri cheese (see page 236)

1 tablespoon freshly squeezed lemon juice

1 teaspoon finely chopped garlic

¾ cup mayonnaise, preferably homemade

2 teaspoons Turkish red pepper paste (see page 244), or 1 teaspoon sweet Hungarian paprika

18 slices basturma (about 6 ounces, see above)

Follow the directions to make the yufka dough, transfer to a zip-top plastic bag, and store at room temperature.

Heat a 12-inch sauté pan over medium heat. Add the olive oil and the cabbage and sauté until it softens, begins to turn translucent, and starts to brown on the edges, about 6 minutes. Season with salt and pepper to taste and set aside to cool.

Slice the onion in half, then slice into very thin half-moons. Put the onion in a mixing bowl, toss with the sumac, and let stand for 10 minutes to lightly pickle the onion.

Combine the cabbage, onion, parsley, oregano, and cheese in a mixing bowl.

Combine the lemon juice and garlic in a small mixing bowl and add a pinch of salt. Let stand for 3 to 5 minutes to lightly pickle the garlic. Stir in the mayonnaise and red pepper paste until you have a creamy sauce.

When you are ready to assemble, put 2 tablespoons of the seasoned mayonnaise on each yufka and smooth it to the edges in a very thin layer. Lay three slices of basturma down the middle of each flatbread. Spoon about ½ cup of the cabbage mixture onto the basturma slices. Fold the left side in towards the middle and then the right side towards the middle, overlapping by about ½ inch, to form a rectangular shape with an open top and bottom. Then fold the other end in towards the middle so that you have a square packet. Rest the gozleme on the folded sides so that they stay together.

When the gozleme are assembled, heat an 11- to 12-inch cast-iron or nonstick pan over medium-low heat. Place three gozleme at a time, seam side down, in the pan. Cook until the filling is hot and the bread is lightly toasted on one side but still soft on the other, about 4 minutes. Flip to the other side and cook 1 minute more. Place on a tray and cover with aluminum foil to keep warm while you cook the remaining four gozleme. Cut in half and serve immediately.

Lamejun, a staple in Armenian cuisine and eaten all over Turkey, translates to "meat with dough." It is a very, very thin flatbread topped with finely chopped beef or lamb, onions, garlic, and spices. The raw topping is put onto the dough so that the juices from the meat and aromatics bake into the flatbread as it cooks. In this recipe, we use all the flavors of a lamejun but skip the meat and let the bread soak up the flavors of olive oil, vegetables, and spice. Top them with yogurt, chopped tomato, and pickled hot peppers and roll them up to eat on the go. ◆ **ANA**

SERVES 6

SUMMER VEGETABLE LAMEJUN

Yufka Dough (page 95)

1 medium to large Italian globe eggplant

Kosher salt

4 tablespoons extra-virgin olive oil

2 cups finely chopped sweet onion, such as Ailsa Craig, Vidalia, or Walla Walla

1½ teaspoons finely chopped garlic

1 tablespoon tomato paste

1 tablespoon Turkish red pepper paste (see page 244)

1½ teaspoons Maras pepper (see page 236)

1½ teaspoons dried spearmint

1 cup finely grated haloumi cheese (see page 234)

1 tablespoon pomegranate molasses (see page 240)

1 teaspoon freshly squeezed lemon juice

Freshly ground black pepper

4 sprigs flat-leaf parsley

8 fresh spearmint leaves

¼ cup finely chopped green onions, mostly the white part

1 tablespoon sumac

½ cup plain whole-milk Greek yogurt

½ cup pickled hot peppers, such as pepperoncini, stemmed

6 lemon wedges

Follow the directions to make the yufka dough, transfer to a zip-top plastic bag, and store at room temperature.

Preheat the oven to 350°F.

Cut the eggplant in half lengthwise and season the cut sides with salt. Brush each cut side with about 1 tablespoon of olive oil. Flip the eggplant over onto a baking sheet. Roast until tender when pressed with a pair of tongs or a spoon, about 40 minutes. You want the eggplant to feel as though it could collapse. Set aside to cool.

Meanwhile, in a small pan over medium-low heat, combine the sweet onions and 1 tablespoon of olive oil and sweat the onions until they are soft and translucent, about 6 minutes. Add the garlic and cook, stirring a couple of times, for 1 minute. Add the tomato paste, red pepper paste, and Maras pepper, and stir to coat the onion.

Transfer the mixture to a food processor fitted with a metal blade. Using a spoon, scrape the eggplant flesh out of the skin and add it to the food processor. Add the mint, haloumi cheese, pomegranate molasses, and lemon juice and pulse until the mixture is coarse but creamy, spreadable, and sticks together when you pick it up with a spoon. Season with salt and black pepper to taste.

When you are ready to assemble, put 4 to 5 tablespoons of the filling on each yufka and smooth it to the edges, until the dough almost disappears.

Line two baking sheets with parchment paper. Place three flatbreads on each baking sheet and bake until the edges are crisp but the lamejun is still soft enough to roll without cracking, about 8 minutes.

Divide the parsley, mint leaves, and green onions among the lamejun and sprinkle each with ½ teaspoon sumac. Dollop each with a spoonful of yogurt and serve folded in half or rolled up, with pepperoncini and a lemon wedge.

Traditional za'atar bread, also known as manoushe, is the daily bread of many Eastern Mediterranean countries. In Lebanon, the dough is stretched out by hand and flipped with a large pillow onto a saj, or domed griddle, to cook. Za'atar is generously spread all over the dough, which is then topped with olive oil and served wrapped in paper by street vendors. It holds a similar place in the hearts of Lebanese people that the simit does in Turkey, as part of a sofra. This type of nationally treasured street food is unique to Middle Eastern culture. Za'atar bread is traditionally served with Pickled Hakurei Turnips (page 210), fresh mint, cucumber, and tomato. ◆ **MAURA**

MAKES 6

ZA'ATAR BREAD

Dough

1 cup warm water, plus more as needed

2¼ teaspoons active dry yeast

2 tablespoons honey

3 cups all-purpose flour

1½ teaspoons kosher salt

2 tablespoons extra-virgin olive oil

Topping

½ to ¾ cup extra-virgin olive oil

½ to ¾ cup za'atar (see page 245)

Kosher salt

Combine the water, yeast, and honey in the bowl of a stand mixer and whisk by hand. Set aside until foamy, 5 minutes.

Add the flour, salt, and olive oil. Using the dough hook, knead on low speed until a smooth dough is formed, 5 minutes. If the dough is a little stiff, you may need to add an additional 1 to 2 tablespoons water.

Remove the dough from the bowl and, using your hands, knead into a smooth ball. Place in a clean, lightly oiled bowl. Cover with plastic wrap and let rise at room temperature until doubled in size, about 1 hour.

Divide the dough into six equal pieces. Lightly flour a work surface and place the balls of dough on the work surface to rest. Cover with plastic wrap and let rise for 45 minutes.

Lightly flour a work surface. Brush a baking sheet with 2 tablespoons olive oil.

Roll each ball into a 5- to 6-inch circle and place on the prepared baking sheet. Brush each dough circle with olive oil, sprinkle with a generous tablespoon of za'atar, and drizzle with a tablespoon of olive oil. Lightly salt each za'atar bread.

Cover with plastic wrap and set aside to rise for 20 to 30 minutes. The dough should spring back when you touch it with your finger.

Preheat the oven to 400°F.

Bake the breads until they just start to brown around the edges, 10 to 12 minutes. These are best served warm.

SAVORY PIES

From the well-known spanakopita, or spinach pie, from Greece to the slipper-shaped pies filled with meat, cheese, and egg called pide in Turkey, we are always overwhelmed and amazed at the variations of savory pies we find throughout the Mediterranean—particularly in Lebanon and Turkey. In Lebanon we tasted baked kibbeh, a tray or cake pan stuffed with a layer of meat and pine nuts, and sliced like a pie.

In Turkey we sampled at least two dozen variations of boreks, which are baked or fried pies made from yufka dough in different shapes and sizes, with different textures and fillings. When Ana visits Istanbul she can't stop herself from an afternoon street-food snack of su borek or Cheese Borek (page 119), a pie that resembles lasagna or kugel with layers of butter, cheese, sometimes yogurt and egg, and yufka dough. It comes hot off a special warming tray, chopped into pieces so you can eat on the go. It tastes of tart yogurt, fresh cheese, and butter with dueling crisp and soft dumpling-like textures from soaking the pastry sheets in a savory custard, layering them, and baking them until crisp on the outside but soft on the inside.

Sofra is the perfect laboratory for putting pastry and savory together, and we are always looking for new variations. Here are a few of our tried and true favorites.

Borek is a pie or pastry that probably originated in Eastern Europe and came to Turkey with the Ottomans. It is made with yufka dough, a thin, almost phyllolike pastry. There are numerous varieties of borek; some are filled with meat, others with cheese, and still others with vegetables. Borek can be rolled, folded, stuffed, twisted, or layered in a baking pan, like this one. This recipe is called su borek, which means "water pastry," probably referring to the boiled-noodle texture resulting from layering and soaking the pie in yogurt and egg until the center becomes almost like a kugel, lasagna, or dumpling, while the top becomes crisp. I prefer to use store-bought yufka in this recipe because it is thinner than both of the yufka recipes in this book. If you want to make it yourself, use the recipe given on page 19 for katmer and roll it out as thin as possible. If you have leftovers, cut the cold borek into small pieces and crisp them in a pan for a perfect afternoon snack or breakfast item. ◆ **ANA**

SERVES 10 TO 12

CHEESE BOREK WITH NIGELLA SEEDS

1 stick (4 ounces) unsalted butter, melted

1½ cups whole milk

¾ cup plain whole-milk Greek yogurt

1 teaspoon kosher salt

2 eggs plus 2 egg yolks

4 sheets store-bought yufka pastry, weighing about 2 pounds (many brands of yufka are available online)

4 (4-ounce) balls buffalo milk mozzarella, grated

3 tablespoons all-purpose flour

2 tablespoons nigella seeds

Preheat the oven to 425°F. Butter an 8-inch square baking dish or an 11 by 7-inch baking pan with 1 tablespoon of the melted butter.

In a small mixing bowl, whisk together the milk, yogurt, salt, and whole eggs until very smooth. Whisk in the remaining 7 tablespoons of melted butter.

Cut the yufka so that you have about eight large pieces that cover the bottom of the pan. It's okay if they don't fit the pan perfectly or if the edges hang over; you can fold everything over the top at the end of assembling.

Place one layer of yufka on the bottom of the pan and brush lavishly with the milk mixture. Repeat until you have four layers of brushed pastry. Distribute the mozzarella over the top of the four soaked yufka layers. Place another four layers of yufka over the cheese filling, brushing with the milk mixture between every layer.

Using a small knife, cut the borek, scoring the pastry so that the custard seeps into the cuts. Make 10 to 12 cuts. It doesn't matter if it breaks up the pastry; you can press it back down with your hands. You don't need to worry about doing it neatly; the cuts will disappear while the borek bakes.

❯ ❯ ❯

▸ ▸ ▸ CHEESE BOREK WITH NIGELLA SEEDS

Mix the remaining milk mixture with the egg yolks and flour. Pour over the top and let soak for 20 minutes. Eventually, the liquid soaks into the pie, so don't worry if it seems like a lot. Sprinkle the top with the nigella seeds.

Place the borek in the oven and lower the heat to 350°F. Bake for about 50 minutes, until golden on top and puffy. Let rest for 15 minutes before slicing and serving.

The word *kibbeh* in Arabic and the word *kofte* in Turkish and Armenian refer to a bulgur wheat dumpling when made with vegetables, or a meatball when made with meat. My version uses a carrot puree that is thickened by fine bulgur wheat until it forms a dough that can be baked, steamed, fried, or stuffed. At Sofra we have a lot of carrots from October until March grown on my husband's farm, Siena Farms, in Sudbury, Massachusetts. The orange color and sweet flavor of fall carrots make an excellent carrot kibbeh stuffed with chopped Swiss chard, pine nuts, garlic, and raisins. This version of kibbeh is baked and steamed, which gives it the consistency of a dumpling: soft, pliable, and with a creamy center. ◆ **ANA**

SERVES 10 TO 12

CARROT KIBBEH WITH GOLDEN RAISINS AND PINE NUTS

5 tablespoons extra-virgin olive oil, plus more if needed

1½ pounds carrots, peeled and cut into 1- to 2-inch chunks

¼ cup Brown Butter (page 213)

1 onion, finely chopped

1 medium green bell pepper, stemmed, seeded, and finely chopped

2 teaspoons sweet Hungarian paprika

1 teaspoon tomato paste

1½ cups fine-ground bulgur wheat

Kosher salt and freshly ground black pepper

2 bunches Swiss chard, stemmed, leaves coarsely chopped, stalks discarded

2 cloves garlic, finely chopped

½ cup golden raisins

½ cup pine nuts, lightly toasted

1 cup plain whole-milk Greek yogurt

Preheat the oven to 375°F. Brush a 9-inch square baking dish or an 11 by 7-inch baking pan with 1 tablespoon of the olive oil.

Put the carrots in a heavy saucepan over medium heat and cover with water. Bring the water to a boil, lower the heat, and simmer until the carrots are very tender when squeezed with a pair of tongs, about 25 minutes. Drain.

Combine the carrots and 1 tablespoon of the Brown Butter in a food processor fitted with a metal blade and puree until very smooth. You should have about 2 cups.

Combine the onion, bell pepper, and 2 tablespoons of the olive oil in a medium saucepan over medium heat and sweat the vegetables until they are soft and translucent but not brown, about 8 minutes. Stir in the paprika and the tomato paste. Stir in 2 cups of the carrot puree and cook until heated, 3 to 5 minutes. Lower the heat to low and stir in the bulgur wheat.

Remove from the heat, cover, and set aside for 15 minutes. The mixture should be soft, like dough. Season with salt and pepper to taste and stir in the remaining 3 tablespoons of Brown Butter. Stir the dough vigorously with a wooden spoon for about 5 minutes, until the dough is soft and very smooth. The goal is to get the mixture as smooth and creamy as possible. Set aside to cool.

In a sauté pan over medium heat, sweat the chard with the remaining 2 tablespoons of olive oil until it wilts, 2 to 3 minutes. Add 2 tablespoons water to the pan to lower the heat, cover, and steam the chard for 1 minute. Stir in the garlic, raisins, and pine nuts and cook until the chard is tender and all the water has evaporated from the pan, 4 to 6 minutes. Season with salt to taste.

Place half the carrot kibbeh in the prepared pan. Using your hands, press it into the pan, forming an even layer all the way to the edges. Use a little olive oil on your hands if it's sticking. Distribute the yogurt as evenly as possible by dolloping it in the middle and spreading it out to the sides. Top with the chard filling and then press the rest of the carrot bulgur mixture onto the top by flattening some in your hands and laying it over the filling. You can roll any edges over and press them into the top piece, sealing the pie by pressing it all together.

Bake until it rises a little and is hot all the way through, about 30 minutes. Set aside to cool for 15 minutes. Cut into 10 to 12 equal portions.

COOK'S NOTE The carrot puree can be made up to 3 days ahead of time so that the assembly goes faster. This is delicious as is or served with labne (page 234) or Tomato–Brown Butter (page 214).

This recipe was inspired by a traditional Greek yogurt and semolina custard that is baked in grape leaves. It is a version of dolma, which means "stuffed" in both Turkish and Greek and is often associated with grape leaves that are stuffed with rice and rolled like short cigars. I love this version because the grape leaves get crispy and a little caramelized, a nice combination with the briny flavor of the leaves. ◆ **ANA**

SERVES 4 TO 6

LAMB AND GRAPE LEAF TARTS WITH ORZO AND SPICY FETA

12 large jarred grape leaves or fresh in the early summer

1 cup finely chopped leek, white part only

⅓ cup finely chopped carrot (about 1 small carrot)

¼ cup plus 1 tablespoon extra-virgin olive oil, plus more as needed

3 cloves garlic, finely chopped

¾ cup cooked orzo

1 pound ground lamb

¾ teaspoon kosher salt

½ teaspoon freshly ground black pepper

1 tablespoon tomato paste

1½ teaspoons ground cumin

Grated zest of 1 orange

1 tablespoon dried oregano, or 1 teaspoon chopped fresh rosemary

1 teaspoon Maras pepper, plus more to serve (see page 236)

2 tablespoons chopped fresh flat-leaf parsley leaves

Juice of ½ orange

1 tablespoon honey

1 cup crumbled sheep's or goat's milk feta

3 tablespoons hot or just-boiled water

1 tablespoon coarsely chopped jalapeño or pickled pepperoncini, stemmed

Preheat the oven to 400°F. Lightly grease four 4-inch tart pans or 6 cups in a muffin tin with olive oil.

Bring a pot of water to a boil, add the grape leaves, and cook for 1 minute. Drain and set aside to cool.

When the grape leaves are cool enough to handle, use a paring knife or a pair of scissors to cut off the remaining stem.

Sweat the leek and carrot in a small sauté pan over medium-low heat in 1 tablespoon olive oil until the vegetables have softened without browning, 5 minutes. Stir in the garlic and cook for 1 more minute. Transfer to a mixing bowl and set aside to cool.

Stir in the orzo, ground lamb, salt, pepper, tomato paste, cumin, orange zest, dried oregano, Maras pepper, and parsley. Use your hands to get everything incorporated.

In a small bowl, combine the orange juice, honey, and the remaining 4 tablespoons of olive oil. Brush one side of the grape leaves with the honey mixture and lay three leaves, brushed side down, into the tart pans, overlapping them a little so that some of the leaves hang over the pan by about 2 inches. Fill with about 1 cup of the meat mixture and fold the leaves over to cover the top. Press the pie into the tart pan so that it molds to the pan. Repeat with the remaining three pies. If you are using a muffin tin, use 2 leaves per pie and divide the lamb mixture into six pies instead of four.

Brush the tops with the remaining honey mixture.

➤ ➤ ➤

LAMB AND GRAPE LEAF TARTS
WITH ORZO AND SPICY FETA

Bake until the grape leaves are crispy on the top and the meat is cooked through, 12 to 15 minutes.

Meanwhile, combine the feta, hot water, and jalapeño or pickled peppers in a blender and blend until very smooth and creamy. Scrape into a small serving bowl and set aside.

Remove the tarts by inverting each onto a plate. Top each serving with a tablespoon of spicy feta sauce.

COOK'S NOTE You can bake these tarts ahead of time and just before serving, crisp them up in a nonstick pan using a teaspoon or so of olive oil.

This recipe for borek, a cigar-shaped pie, is delicious with seasonal vegetable combinations like fresh peas and green onions in the spring or butternut squash and leeks in the fall. The soft texture of the dough also makes it easy to sop up the tomato brown–butter and warm garlicky yogurt, the two sauces we serve with these. The flavors come alive with a great balance of tart sumac, warm mint, and sweet heat from the Turkish red pepper flakes. I prefer to use store-bought yufka in this recipe because it is almost as thin as phyllo and it's hard to do this by hand. If you want to make it yourself, use the katmer recipe given on page 19. ◆ **ANA**

SERVES 8

VEGETABLE BOREK WITH WARM GARLICKY YOGURT

1 cup chopped leek, white part only, or sweet onion such Ailsa Craig, Vidalia, or Walla Walla

2 tablespoons extra-virgin olive oil

3 cups peeled and grated butternut squash, or peeled and grated kohlrabi or grated zucchini (see Note, page 129)

4 to 5 ounces grated haloumi cheese or crumbled barrel-aged Greek feta cheese

1½ teaspoons kosher salt, plus more as needed

Freshly ground black pepper

1 teaspoon Baharat Spice (page 221)

1 heaping teaspoon finely chopped garlic

1 teaspoon freshly squeezed lemon juice

2 cups plain whole-milk Greek yogurt

1 tablespoon butter

16 sheets store-bought yufka, preferably triangles

2 cups Tomato–Brown Butter (page 214)

1 tablespoon sumac

1 tablespoon dried spearmint

2 teaspoons Maras pepper (see page 236)

In a skillet over medium-low heat, sweat the leek in 1 tablespoon olive oil stirring until the leek is soft and translucent but not brown, about 5 minutes.

If you are using grated kohlrabi or zucchini, lightly salt it and let it sit for 5 minutes to draw the water out of it. Squeeze small amounts between the palms of your hands, getting as much water out of it as possible.

Otherwise, to make the filling, combine the grated squash, leek, cheese, salt, pepper, and Baharat Spice in a bowl. Test a little of the filling for seasoning by frying a small patty in oil. The saltiness will vary depending on the saltiness of the cheese; adjust the seasoning as needed.

To make the garlicky yogurt, combine the garlic, lemon juice, and a pinch of salt in a small mixing bowl and set aside for 5 minutes to soften the flavor of the raw garlic. Stir in the yogurt and season with salt and pepper to taste.

Preheat the oven to 400°F. Butter a large, heavy baking sheet or spray it with nonstick cooking spray.

Place 2 to 3 tablespoons of the filling onto the large end of a pastry triangle and roll it up tightly like a cigar. Roll it as tightly as possible without breaking it so that the borek is compact and stays together after it is baked. Brush a little bit of the garlicky yogurt on the tip end of the triangle to help seal the roll. Place the borek on the baking sheet. Repeat to use all the pastry and filling. Brush each borek with garlicky yogurt (you should use about ½ cup for brushing).

Bake until the borek are lightly browned and baked through, 30 to 35 minutes. Set aside to cool. Keep the yogurt out at room temperature while they are baking until you are ready to serve.

Trim off the ends of the borek cigar and split them down the center lengthwise. The filling is exposed, but you will place them cut side down into the dish to bake again so they will look like skinny cigars.

When you are ready to serve, spoon the Tomato–Brown Butter on the bottom of a 9 by 13-baking dish. Arrange the borek side by side in the pan as you would a baked pasta dish, with the cut side down, and spread the remaining garlicky yogurt on top. Warm the borek in the oven until the sauce on the bottom is bubbly and the borek are hot through the center, 5 to 10 minutes. Drizzle with the remaining 1 tablespoon of olive oil and sprinkle the sumac, mint, and Maras pepper evenly over the top. Serve hot.

COOK'S NOTE Grate the squash or kohlrabi on the large holes of a box grater. If you are using zucchini, lightly salt it and let it stand in a colander for 5 minutes to release some water. Squeeze the zucchini between your palms until most of the water is gone.

This style of borek was inspired by a photo of beet pies that I saw on the Instagram feed of chef Sami Tamimi of *Jerusalem* fame. He used kataifi pastry to wrap an eggplant filling before baking it. This is not a typical style of borek but is a deliciously buttery, crisp, and fun way to present it. Traditionally, kataifi pastry is used in baklava-style desserts in place of phyllo dough. It resembles phyllo that has been finely shredded. It's made from a batter that is poured through a container in which there are fine holes. The streams of thin batter flow onto a spinning hot metal plate and cook quickly. They are pulled off the hot plate like a lock of hair and look very much like vermicelli. You can prepare this recipe without the chicken to make it vegetarian, and you can vary the size of the borek depending on how you are serving them. ◆ **ANA**

SERVES 8

CHICKEN AND WALNUT BOREK

12 ounces boneless, skinless chicken thighs

1 teaspoon kosher salt, plus more to taste

Freshly ground black pepper

4 tablespoons extra-virgin olive oil

1 teaspoon dried oregano

1 cup chopped leeks, white part only

½ stick (2 ounces) unsalted butter

⅓ cup lightly toasted walnut pieces, plus 2 tablespoons for garnish

¾ cup grated kasseri (see page 236) or Gruyère cheese

½ cup peeled and grated candy-striped beets

2 tablespoons finely chopped green onions, mostly the white parts

2 tablespoons finely chopped fresh flat-leaf parsley leaves

2 tablespoons plain whole-milk Greek yogurt

1 teaspoon freshly squeezed lemon juice

½ (16-ounce) box of kataifi pastry (see page 236)

Preheat the oven to 375°F.

Season the chicken thighs with ¾ teaspoon of the salt and ½ teaspoon pepper. Rub with 1 tablespoon of the olive oil and the oregano and place in a baking dish in a single layer. Add ½ cup water and braise in the oven, uncovered, until the thighs are tender when squeezed with a pair of tongs, about 25 minutes.

When the chicken is cool enough to handle, finely chop and put in a mixing bowl.

In a small sauté pan over medium-low heat, sweat the leeks in 1 tablespoon butter and 1 tablespoon water (so that they don't brown) until they are soft and silky, 5 to 6 minutes. Add to the chicken.

Stir in the walnuts, grated cheese, grated beets, green onions, parsley, and yogurt. Stir in the lemon juice and season the filling with salt and pepper to taste.

Melt the remaining 3 tablespoons of butter and stir in the remaining 3 tablespoons of olive oil.

Open the package of kataifi and cut the "rope" in half so that it's easier to work with. Place one-half back in the plastic and freeze it for future use.

Pull some strands of kataifi equal to about a ¼ inch in diameter, lay them onto a flat surface, and spread them out a little so that you have "strips" of shredded pastry (see photos, right). Continue to pull strips of the shredded pastry until you have sixteen strips that are ¼ inch in diameter. If your work surface is not that big, you can do eight strips at a time and keep the pastry covered with a clean

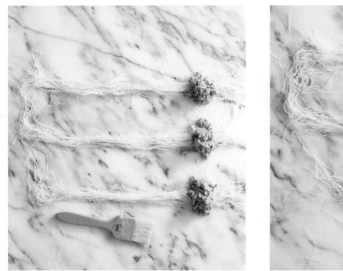

towel or plastic wrap while you work with one at a time. Brush the strips of strands generously with the butter and oil mixture. Place 2 tablespoons of filling on each strip, 1 inch from the end.

Roll the pastries up around the filling so that you have something that looks like a nest enveloping the filling. It's okay if the top and bottom of the nests are open; you want the filling exposed a little. Turn the nests filling side up and place them on a baking sheet. When you have all sixteen rolled and on the baking sheet, brush them again with any remaining oil and butter mixture.

Bake until golden brown and crisp on the outside, 25 minutes.

Sprinkle the remaining 2 tablespoons walnuts over the top of the nests and serve warm or at room temperature.

This is a large version of the classic spinach pie, and a Sofra holiday specialty. Working in a bakery has given me the opportunity to play with savory pastries, which I almost never get to do as a restaurant pastry chef. I love exploring the popular savory breads and pastries of Middle Eastern countries because the flavor combinations often startle and inspire. I am lucky to have Ana to turn to as a resource for my ideas. Here we present her recipe for the filling combined with my method of making spanakopita, I've added two of Ana's favorite herbs, dried spearmint and oregano. The serpentine is formed by rolling the filled logs into the shape of a snake. ◆ **MAURA**

SERVES 6 TO 8

SPANAKOPITA SERPENTINE

Filling

1½ pounds fresh spinach

2 tablespoons extra-virgin olive oil

1 white onion, finely chopped

1 bunch finely chopped green onions, mostly the white part

1 large bulb fennel, minced

1 clove garlic, finely chopped

12 ounces crumbled feta cheese

¾ cup labne (see page 233) or plain whole-milk Greek yogurt

¼ cup chopped fresh flat-leaf parsley leaves

1 teaspoon dried spearmint

½ teaspoon dried oregano

Kosher salt and freshly ground black pepper

Assembly

About 4 ounces/6 sheets phyllo dough (see Working with Phyllo, page 135)

¼ cup clarified butter (page 215)

1 egg, whisked

Fill a small bowl with ice and water. Line a baking sheet with paper towels. Line a second baking sheet with parchment paper.

To make the filling, bring a large pot of water to a boil over high heat and add a pinch of salt. Add the spinach and cook until soft and wilted, 1 minute. Drain into a colander and then transfer to the bowl of ice water. Set aside until cooled completely.

Drain the spinach again. Squeeze out as much water as possible and then place on the paper towel–lined baking sheet to continue draining. Coarsely chop.

Remove the phyllo from the refrigerator to warm up a bit so that it is easy to unfold without cracking.

Place a large skillet over medium heat and add the olive oil. Add the white onion, green onions, fennel, and garlic and sauté until soft, about 8 minutes. Set aside to cool.

In a large bowl, combine the feta cheese, labne, parsley, spearmint, oregano, and spinach. Stir in the onion mixture and mix until well combined. Add salt and pepper to taste.

Preheat the oven to 375°F. Place the sides of an 8-inch springform pan (without a bottom) on the parchment paper–lined baking sheet.

To assemble the serpentine, lay the phyllo out on a work surface and cover with a dry towel. Place one sheet of parchment paper large enough to hold one sheet of phyllo next to the phyllo to work on.

Place one sheet of phyllo, with the longer side facing you, on the parchment paper. Lightly butter the first sheet. Place another sheet on top and lightly butter it. Fold the phyllo in half from the top.

❯ ❯ ❯

SPANAKOPITA SERPENTINE

Place about one-third of the spinach filling in a thin line across the edge closest to you. Roll into a loose log. Starting at the left end, roll it around into a coil shape. Place on the prepared baking sheet. Butter the next two sheets of phyllo, folding them in half the same way and placing one-third of the filling across the bottom edge. Roll into a loose log. Place this log at the end of the coiled phyllo on the baking sheet, and roll the logs around one another to continue to enlarge the coil shape (see photo, page 132). Repeat with the final two sheets of phyllo and filling. Place that log on the baking sheet at the end of the last roll to continue the coil.

Place the springform ring on the baking sheet and snap it around the finished serpentine. Brush the top of the serpentine with the whisked egg.

Bake until the top is crispy and golden brown, 40 to 45 minutes. Remove the springform ring immediately. Set aside to cool.

Serve warm or at room temperature.

COOK'S NOTE It works best to put the springform pan directly on a parchment paper–lined baking sheet instead of using the bottom of the pan. Otherwise the serpentine will sit in too much melted butter as it bakes.

WORKING WITH PHYLLO Packaged phyllo comes in 1-pound packages that contain either two 8-ounce sleeves of smaller sheets or one sleeve of larger sheets. All of the recipes in this book are made with the larger sheets which are commonly 14 by 18 inches. It is most often available in the freezer section.

Be sure to thaw phyllo in the refrigerator the night before you plan to use it. Remove it from the refrigerator 5 minutes before needed; it is important that it softens a bit before you unroll the package to prevent it from cracking. You can use the broken pieces in the center layers of spanakopita or baklava.

Prepare your work surface first. Place the phyllo sheets on one side, and cover with parchment paper and a barely damp towel to prevent them from drying out. Place another sheet of parchment paper directly next to the phyllo to butter and build the phyllo sheets on. It is best to use clarified butter (page 215) and to keep the butter just warm for the thinnest layer of butter possible. Using a pastry brush, brush the first layers very sparingly, but make sure to thoroughly brush the top layer, so it becomes crispy and nicely colored. Generously butter the baking pan. If you have any unused phyllo sheets, wrap them in plastic, return to the box, and refrigerate.

Here I have turned the traditional Turkish Simit (page 43) into a filled loaf. What I love about simit is the crunchy-sweet exterior and the softness of the dough, so I wanted to contrast that with a cheesey filling. Even filled and braided, the simit keeps its sweet, crunchy crust. It goes beautifully with the salty feta and za'atar almond filling. I love seeing it on a holiday table, but I'll also eat it as a meal served with a salad. ◆ **MAURA**

SERVES 6 TO 8

STUFFED SIMIT

1 cup room-temperature water

2 teaspoons active dry yeast

2 teaspoons sugar

2¼ cups all-purpose flour

1 teaspoon kosher salt

8 ounces crumbled feta cheese

½ cup Za'atar Spiced Almonds (page 229)

½ cup toasted sesame seeds (see page 241)

Grape molasses (pekmez) (see page 233), for brushing braid

To make the dough, in the bowl of a stand mixer, whisk, by hand, ¼ cup of the water, the yeast, and the sugar. Set aside until frothy, 5 minutes.

Add the flour, salt, and remaining ¾ cup water to the bowl. Using a dough hook, mix on medium-low speed until a smooth elastic dough forms, 8 to 10 minutes. Scrape the sides of the bowl and use your hands to form into a ball. Cover with plastic wrap and let rest until doubled in size, about 1 hour.

Lightly flour a work surface. Line a baking sheet with parchment paper.

Place the dough on the prepared work surface. Roll the dough into a 6- by 12-inch rectangle. Carefully score the rectangle into thirds. Do not cut through the dough; the marks will be the guide. Cut each outside third of the dough on a downward angle into six strips.

Spread the crumbled feta down the center of the rectangle. Sprinkle the za'atar almonds evenly on top of the feta. Beginning at the top, take each cut strip and slightly stretch it out, crossing them over the feta filling and alternating sides, creating a braided pattern across the top and sealing in the filling. Carefully lift and place the braid on a prepared baking sheet.

Preheat the oven to 375°F.

Brush the braided loaf lightly with the grape molasses and coat completely with sesame seeds. Cover with plastic wrap and let rise at room temperature for 30 minutes.

Bake until golden brown, about 35 minutes. Set aside to cool on the baking sheet. This is best served the day it is made.

Fatayer, a Lebanese tart, is usually made with a yeasted dough, but instead we use our Crick Crack dough as a tart shell. This is a very easy filling that makes a great breakfast, appetizer, or even dessert with fresh fruit. It is best to purchase ground walnuts for this recipe instead of chopping walnut halves; they blend better with the grated manouri, especially for a hand pie. Other great fillings include sesame-walnut filling (see page 97) or Whipped Goat Cheese with Almonds and Golden Raisins (page 59). ◆ **MAURA**

MAKES 9 TARTS

CHEESE AND HONEY FATAYER

Crick Crack dough (page 97)

2 tablespoons yellow cornmeal

1½ cups grated manouri cheese

¾ cup toasted ground walnuts

¼ cup honey, preferably raw, plus more for drizzling

MANOURI CHEESE
Manouri is a very mild Greek cheese, often referred to as saltless feta because it is made from the whey drained during the process of making feta cheese. It is creamier than feta because cream is added to the whey, making its soft texture perfect for this tart.

Lightly flour a work surface. Line a baking sheet with parchment paper.

Roll the Crick Crack dough into a 12- by 12-inch square that is ⅛ inch thick. Cut out 8 to 9 (4-inch) circles. Do not reroll the scraps; the resulting dough will shrink too much. You can, however, bake the scraps off to snack on as crackers. Place each dough circle on the prepared baking sheet, wrap in plastic wrap, and let rest in the refrigerator for 1 hour.

Preheat the oven to 350°F. Line a baking sheet with parchment paper. Lightly sprinkle a work surface with the cornmeal. In a small bowl, mix the manouri, walnuts, and honey until well combined.

Place the dough circles on the cornmeal (to prevent sticking and create a nice crunch on the fatayer). Place 2 tablespoons of the cheese mixture in the center of each dough circle. To form a triangle, fold the left and right sides of the circle up against the sides of the filling, making them meet at the top of the circle, at 12 o'clock. Fold the right side down first and the left side on top to make a sealed point at the top. Fold the side closest to you against the filling, forming a triangle, then press to seal both sides. Repeat with all the dough and filling.

Bake until the shells begin to brown, 15 to 20 minutes. Serve warm, drizzled with honey. If the honey is too thick to drizzle, you can loosen it by placing it in a warm water bath.

In Turkey, pide is a very popular flatbread, folded into a slipper shape to hold the filling. This meat- or vegetable-stuffed snack is a Turkish comfort food prepared in small shops across Istanbul that are similar to our pizza shops. The long pies are shaped with ease, slid into a wood-fired oven, and brushed with melted butter before serving. ◆ **MAURA**

SERVES 6

SPICY LAMB PIDE

Dough

½ cup warm water

1 teaspoon active dry yeast

1 tablespoon honey

1½ cups all-purpose flour

¾ teaspoon kosher salt

2 tablespoons extra-virgin olive oil

Filling

12 ounces ground lamb

1 small onion, minced

2 teaspoons Baharat Spice (page 221)

1 teaspoon dried spearmint

1 tablespoon Maras pepper (see page 236)

2 tablespoons tomato paste

2 teaspoons Turkish red pepper paste (see page 244)

1 clove garlic, finely chopped

1½ tablespoons pomegranate molasses (see page 240)

¼ cup finely chopped green onions, green part only

¾ cup grated kasseri cheese (see page 236)

¼ stick (1 ounce) unsalted butter, melted

To prepare the dough, combine the water, yeast, and honey in the bowl of a stand mixer. Whisk, by hand, to combine. Set aside until foamy, 5 minutes.

Add the flour, salt, and 1 tablespoon of the olive oil. Using the dough hook, knead on low speed until a smooth dough forms, 5 minutes. If the dough is a little stiff, you may need to add an additional 1 to 2 tablespoons water.

Remove the dough from the bowl and, using your hands, knead into a smooth ball. Place in a clean, lightly oiled bowl; cover with plastic wrap and let rise at room temperature until doubled in size, about 1 hour.

Prepare the lamb filling while the dough is resting. Place a large skillet over medium heat. Add the lamb, onion, Baharat Spice, mint, and Maras pepper and cook until the onion is soft and the lamb is lightly browned, about 8 minutes.

Add the tomato paste, red pepper paste, and garlic. Lower the heat and cook until dry, 5 to 8 minutes. Set aside to cool. Add the pomegranate molasses, green onions, and kasseri. The lamb filling can be prepared up to 3 days in advance and stored in the refrigerator.

Preheat the oven to 400°F. Line a baking sheet with parchment paper. Lightly flour a work surface.

Turn the dough onto the prepared surface, pressing it into a rectangle. Gently roll it into a 15- by 7-inch rectangle and place on the prepared baking sheet. Use a fork or dough docker to pierce holes over the surface of the dough; this will help the dough rise evenly around the lamb. Spoon the lamb filling down the center of the rectangle, leaving 2 inches along both sides and 1 inch at each end. Press the lamb filling so it forms a flat and even layer. Fold each side over the filling. The ends will not meet (see photo, left).Then pinch the ends to seal. Brush lightly with the remaining 1 tablespoon of olive oil. Bake until golden brown, 25 to 30 minutes.

Remove from the oven and immediately brush with the melted butter. Slice into 6 pieces and serve warm.

COOKIES AND CONFECTIONS

There really isn't another sweet that puts a smile on someone's face faster than a cookie does. It can instantly turn your day around or give you a momentary escape. Maura is especially particular when it comes to developing cookie recipes. Hours of thought, trial, and experimentation go into all her cookies; every bite has to satisfy. If you crave a delicate buttery cookie like our Syrian Shortbread, you want it to melt in your mouth. If you want a soft, chewy cookie like the Oatmeal Sesame Cookie, you don't want to be disappointed if it's crunchy.

You will see a number of familiar cookies at Sofra, but Maura's playful and creative side is especially on display when reinventing Middle Eastern sweets. Cookies are a shared experience over there as they are here, an essential element of social events and religious celebrations. They are also just as ubiquitous over there as they are here; storefronts are piled high with sugared Ma'amoul, halvah, and a variety of sesame and pistachio confections.

For these recipes we usually use cold butter instead of room-temperature butter. We prefer to cube it very small to cream it with the sugars. Room-temperature butter can be different every time, so we chill the butter to achieve consistent results.

I think of these cookies as our gateway item, as most people will recognize them if our Arabic ones are unfamiliar to them. It wasn't supposed to happen this way, but these cookies took off and quickly became a neighborhood favorite. Parents bring their children in for them after school, and families and local offices order them by the dozens. This is a fantastic fudgy cookie, and not at all Middle Eastern, but impossible to resist. ◆ **MAURA**

MAKES 2 DOZEN

EARTHQUAKE COOKIES

1¼ cups all-purpose flour

½ cup unsweetened cocoa powder

2 teaspoons baking powder

½ teaspoon fleur de sel or kosher salt

1 stick (4 ounces) unsalted butter, chilled and cut into ¼-inch cubes

1½ cups firmly packed light brown sugar

2 eggs

8 ounces extra-bittersweet chocolate (70% cacao), melted and cooled

1 teaspoon vanilla extract

⅓ cup whole milk

1½ cups confectioners' sugar

1½ cups granulated sugar

Sift together the flour, cocoa powder, baking powder, and salt; set aside.

Combine the butter and brown sugar in the bowl of a stand mixer fitted with a paddle attachment. Mix on medium speed until light and very fluffy, about 5 minutes. Scrape the bowl. Lower the speed and add the eggs one at a time, scraping between additions. Still on low speed, add the chocolate. Mix until well combined, about 1 minute. Add the vanilla to the milk. Staying at low speed, alternate adding the flour mixture and the milk. Begin and end with the flour mixture in three additions, scraping the bowl between additions.

Transfer the dough, which will resemble a very wet batter, to a bowl; cover and refrigerate at least overnight, and up to 1 week.

Preheat the oven to 350°F. Line a baking sheet with parchment paper. Put the confectioners' sugar and the granulated sugar in separate bowls.

Use a 2-tablespoon cookie scoop or portion scoop to shape the cookies. Roll each scoop into the granulated sugar first and then into the confectioners' sugar, coating completely.

Place the cookies onto the prepared baking sheet ½ inch apart. Bake until puffed and cracked and just set around the edges, 14 to 16 minutes. The centers will still be soft and appear underbaked. Cool completely on the baking sheet. Serve right away or store in an airtight container for up to 4 days.

Tahini is nutty and smooth like peanut butter, and it adds a surprise layer of savory depth greater than what you get from traditional nut butters. A few years ago I became obsessed with adding it to desserts, and I thought that it would work well in an oatmeal cookie, so I began experimenting to find the perfect combination. By adding a few more flavors like cardamom and halvah (a sesame confection made with tahini and sugar syrup), I came up with a Sofra version of the classic oatmeal cookie. ◆ **MAURA**

MAKES 2 DOZEN

OATMEAL SESAME COOKIES

3 cups old-fashioned rolled oats

1½ cups all-purpose flour

1½ teaspoons baking soda

1 teaspoon kosher salt

1 teaspoon ground cardamom

1 tablespoon crumbled halvah (see page 234)

2 tablespoons toasted sesame seeds (see page 241)

2 eggs

1 teaspoon vanilla extract

1¾ sticks (7 ounces) unsalted butter, chilled and cut into ¼-inch cubes

½ cup granulated sugar

1 cup firmly packed light brown sugar

¼ cup tahini (see page 242)

Combine the oats, flour, baking soda, salt, cardamom, halvah, and sesame seeds in a bowl and set aside. Combine the eggs and vanilla extract in another bowl.

Combine the butter, granulated sugar, brown sugar, and tahini in the bowl of a stand mixer fitted with a paddle attachment. Mix on medium speed until smooth and light in color, 5 minutes. Scrape the bowl.

Lower the speed and add the egg mixture. Scrape the sides of the bowl again. Staying on low speed, add the oat mixture and mix until completely incorporated.

Transfer to a clean bowl. Cover and chill until firm, at least 6 hours, or up to overnight. It is important not to use this cookie dough until it is firm.

Preheat the oven to 350°F. Line a baking sheet with parchment paper.

Use a 2-tablespoon cookie scoop or portion scoop to shape the dough into 1½-inch balls. Place on the baking sheet ½ inch apart. Press each ball to flatten just a bit.

Bake the cookies until they appear slightly darkened around edges but still underbaked, 15 to 16 minutes. Cool completely on the baking sheet. Store in an airtight container for up to 4 days.

I came across this recipe in a Lebanese cookbook, and it has become a favorite little candy of mine. It is very similar to our Halawa (page 162), using pistachios and sugar to make a firm paste. The tricky part is grinding the nuts to extract enough oil from them to hold this bar together. It is traditionally served with mascarpone or crème fraîche, but adding white chocolate ganache is the creamiest combination I could think of. It needs a little liquid to keep it together, so I added tangerine juice. As an alternative, you could add part water and part rose water, Moscato, or St. Germain, or try adding a brewed tea like chamomile in place of the juice. ◆ **MAURA**

MAKES 32 PIECES

TANGERINE BOHSALINO WITH WHITE CHOCOLATE GANACHE

1½ cups shelled raw pistachios

½ cup sugar

2 tablespoons freshly squeezed tangerine juice

½ cup heavy cream

Grated zest of 1 tangerine

8 ounces white chocolate, chopped

1 tablespoon unsalted butter

Lightly spray an 8-inch square baking dish with nonstick cooking spray and line with plastic wrap.

Coarsely grind the pistachios in a food processor, then add the sugar and tangerine juice. Keep processing until a soft, malleable paste is formed. Transfer to a bowl. Wet your hands and massage the mixture until you have released enough oil from the nuts to bind the pistachio paste.

Press the paste into the prepared pan in an even layer, using the bottom of a measuring cup and packing the paste as firmly as possible. Cover and refrigerate for at least 30 minutes, or up to 1 week.

Heat the heavy cream with the tangerine zest to just under a boil. Remove from the heat, cover, and let infuse for 30 minutes.

To make the ganache, put the white chocolate and butter in a bowl. Reheat the cream slightly and strain over the bowl of white chocolate. Set aside until the chocolate has softened, 3 to 4 minutes, then stir with a rubber spatula until smooth. Chill the ganache until it starts to firm up but is still pourable, 30 minutes. Pour over the chilled pistachio layer. Refrigerate until firm, about 4 hours.

Lift the plastic wrap to remove the confection from the baking dish. Slice into 1-inch squares. Serve cold.

Each Middle Eastern country has its own version of shortbread, called graybeh (ghray-bay). These are the sugar cookies of Lebanon, Syria, and Morocco. I was immediately drawn to this one because of the clarified butter, which gives them a very delicate, melt-in-your-mouth texture. I make them into thumbprint cookies, but you could also simply scoop them and place a pistachio or whole almond in the center instead. Because they are so delicate, we bake them on two stacked sheet pans to ensure even baking and prevent any coloring. ◆ **MAURA**

MAKES 30

SYRIAN SHORTBREADS

1 cup clarified butter (page 215), refrigerated until soft, 2 to 3 hours

⅔ cup sugar

2 cups all-purpose flour

½ teaspoon kosher salt

⅔ cup jam of your choice

In the bowl of a stand mixer fitted with a paddle attachment, mix the butter and sugar until just combined. The softness of the butter is very important: if it is too liquid, your cookies will spread too much. What you want is called *beurre pommade*, soft like a face cream. Cover and refrigerate until firm, about 2 hours.

Return the sugar mixture to the stand mixer and, using a paddle attachment, beat on medium speed until the mixture is very light and fluffy and has the consistency of whipped cream, 8 minutes. Scrape the sides of the bowl. Add the flour and salt and mix on low speed until smooth. Cover and refrigerate at least overnight, or up to 1 week.

Use a 2-tablespoon cookie scoop or portion scoop to shape the cookies. Place level scoops in a small container or on a baking sheet. Cover and refrigerate for at least 30 minutes.

Using a small melon baller or the rounded back of a teaspoon, scoop out the centers. You can re-form all the centers into new cookies. Cover and refrigerate at least 1 hour, or up to overnight.

Preheat the oven to 300°F. Line a baking sheet with parchment paper and place a second baking sheet under it to prevent the cookies from coloring and to keep them tender.

Place the cookies on the prepared baking sheets about 2 inches apart and fill each center with 1 teaspoon jam. Bake until the cookies are cracked but not changed in color, 25 to 30 minutes.

These are very delicate cookies, too fragile to pick up until cooled. Store in an airtight container for up to 4 days.

COOK'S NOTE I like to chill these baked cookies once they have cooled. I place them right in the refrigerator on the baking sheet, or you can use a spatula to transfer them to a plate. This firms them up because they are so delicate. Once they are firm, remove from the refrigerator and serve at room temperature.

Very simple to make, these cookies are everything in one bite: buttery and crunchy yet tender. These shortbreads work well when you need cookie crumbs for a crust or something to layer with vanilla ice cream and chocolate sauce. They are also the perfect afternoon pick-me-up with coffee, tea, or our Tahini Hot Chocolate (page 206). ◆ **MAURA**

MAKES 2 DOZEN

TAHINI SHORTBREAD COOKIES

1¼ sticks (5 ounces) unsalted butter, at room temperature

¾ cup confectioners' sugar

1 cup tahini (see Cook's Note, below)

1¾ cups all-purpose flour

2 teaspoons kosher salt

½ cup toasted sesame seeds (see page 241)

Lightly flour a work surface.

Combine the butter, confectioners' sugar, and tahini in the bowl of a stand mixer fitted with a paddle attachment. Mix on medium speed until smooth, 4 to 5 minutes. Scrape the bowl. Add the flour and salt and mix on low speed until the dough is smooth.

Transfer the dough to the prepared work surface. Divide the dough in half and knead until smooth. Roll each piece of dough into a log approximately 1 inch in diameter.

Spread ¼ cup sesame seeds onto a small plate. Roll each log in the sesame seeds, coating the log completely. Wrap each log tightly in parchment paper, twisting each end. Refrigerate until firm, at least 4 hours or up to overnight.

Preheat the oven to 300°F. Line a baking sheet with parchment paper.

Slice the logs into ¼-inch-thick coins and place on the prepared baking sheet 2 inches apart.

Bake until firm around the edges and not colored, 12 to 15 minutes. Cool completely on the baking sheet. Store in an airtight container for up to 5 days.

COOK'S NOTE Sometimes tahini has a layer of oil that separates, so be sure to incorporate all the oil into the paste before measuring to prevent this dough from being too crumbly. If there is a visible layer of oil on top, it is easier to combine by pouring the contents of the jar out and stirring to combine. It is especially important in this recipe that the oil is fully incorporated or your cookie will not come together.

Ma'amoul means "filled" in Arabic. These cookies are usually prepared by pressing shortbread dough into special wooden molds and filling them with pistachios, almonds, or dates. They are as common in Middle Eastern countries as chocolate chip cookies are in the U.S. and are used to welcome guests into the home, where they are served with tea. This rolled version was inspired by chef Greg Malouf, a constant source of inspiration and a good friend. Use soft Medjool dates in the filling or date paste, which is sold in blocks in Middle Eastern stores and will save you the trouble of pitting and give you a smoother, easier-to-work-with filling. ◆ **MAURA**

MAKES 2 DOZEN

DATE ESPRESSO MA'AMOUL

Dough

1¾ cups all-purpose flour

6 tablespoons confectioners' sugar

½ teaspoon kosher salt

2 sticks (8 ounces) unsalted butter, chilled and cut into ¼-inch cubes

¼ cup whole milk

2 tablespoons extra-virgin olive oil

1 cup confectioners' sugar, for dusting

Filling

1 cup (9 ounces) pitted and chopped Medjool dates, packed

8 ounces almond paste (see page 231)

1½ teaspoons ground cinnamon

1 tablespoon grated orange zest

¼ cup freshly squeezed orange juice

2 tablespoons brewed espresso or strong coffee

To prepare the dough, combine the flour, confectioners' sugar, and salt in the bowl of a stand mixer. Toss in the cubed butter. Using a paddle attachment, mix on low speed until the butter is in pea-sized pieces, 4 minutes.

Combine the milk and olive oil; add to the dough. Continue to mix on low speed until the dough comes together.

Lightly flour a work surface. Turn the dough out and knead into a rectangle. Divide in half. Wrap each piece with plastic wrap and chill for at least 1 hour, or up to 4 days.

To prepare the filling, coarsely chop the dates and break the almond paste into small pieces by hand into the bowl of a stand mixer. Add the cinnamon, orange zest, orange juice, and espresso. Using a paddle attachment, mix on medium speed until well combined and smooth. The filling can be prepared up to a week in advance and refrigerated.

To form the ma'amoul, bring the filling to room temperature. Lightly flour a work surface. Roll the first half of the dough into a 12- by 6-inch rectangle. With the 12-inch side facing you, spread 1 cup of the date filling in an even layer, leaving a clean ¼-inch edge on the side farthest from you. Gently fold the edge closest to you over about ⅛ inch and continue rolling away from you into a cylinder. Roll gently to thin the log out slightly. With the seam side on the bottom, press the roll so it is flat on the top. Repeat with the remaining dough and filling. Wrap each log and refrigerate until firm, at least 4 hours or up to overnight.

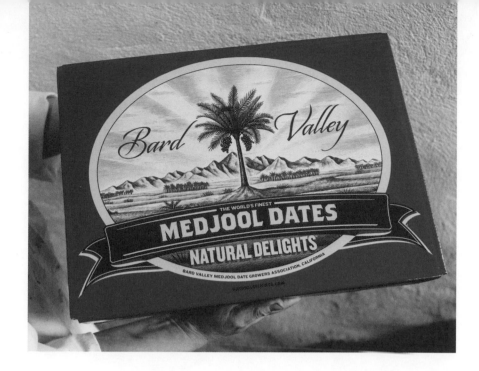

Preheat the oven to 325°F. Line a baking sheet with parchment paper.

Slice the logs at a slight diagonal into ½-inch-thick cookies. Place on the prepared baking sheet about 2 inches apart.

Bake until lightly golden, 25 minutes. Cool completely on the baking sheet. Dust generously with confectioners' sugar. Store in an airtight container for up to 5 days.

COOK'S NOTE Think of oven heat as another ingredient in the recipe. First, preheat the oven properly, for 15 to 20 minutes. Use a small oven thermometer, available in hardware stores, for accuracy. Then, before you make an entire pan of cookies, test by baking two or three first. If necessary, you can adjust the temperature and/or the time on the baked items. It is also wise to rotate the pan halfway through the baking for even baking and browning.

I adapted this cookie from a Greek recipe I found while researching cookies for Easter. I already loved the ma'amoul cookie dough (page 152), so I made it with some semolina flour for added crunch and a slightly more crumbly texture. The dough has become a favorite dough for other fillings, like apple or pistachios. Because you are using a small amount of filling in each cookie, it is best to purchase ground walnuts for this recipe. I am a fan of using traditional wooden ma'amoul molds, like the ones you might see throughout the Middle East. If you see them at a Middle Eastern store or online, buy them and the cookies you make with them will be very special. The other option for shaping them is to make a very simple crescent shape, which I have included here. ◆ **MAURA**

MAKES 15

MARZIPAN COOKIES WITH FIGS AND WALNUTS

1 cup ground walnuts

½ cup fig jam, such as Mymouné brand or other loose jam

1 tablespoon honey

2 ounces almond paste (see page 231)

1¼ cups plus 2 tablespoons all-purpose flour

6 tablespoons fine semolina

6 tablespoons confectioners' sugar, plus more for dusting

½ teaspoon kosher salt

2 sticks (8 ounces) unsalted butter, chilled and cut into ¼-inch cubes

2 tablespoons extra-virgin olive oil

¼ cup whole milk

Preheat the oven to 350°F.

Spread the walnuts on a baking sheet. Bake until lightly toasted, about 8 minutes.

Combine the toasted walnuts, fig jam, and honey in a small bowl. Break the almond paste up into small pieces and add to the walnut mixture. Using the back of a spoon, mix until moistened and bound together.

Combine the flour, semolina, confectioners' sugar, salt, and butter in the bowl of a stand mixer fitted with a paddle attachment. Mix on low speed until the butter is in pea-size pieces.

Combine the olive oil and milk in a small bowl. Add to the flour mixture and mix until completely combined.

Lightly flour a work surface.

Transfer the dough to the work surface and knead until smooth. Divide the dough in half. Wrap each piece in plastic wrap and refrigerate until firm, at least 1 hour, or up to overnight.

Lightly flour a work surface. Line a baking sheet with parchment paper.

Bring the dough to room temperature if it has been chilled overnight. Roll out into a 12-inch square that is ⅛ inch thick. Using a 3-inch round cutter, cut out circles. Reroll the scraps to form more circles. Repeat with the remaining dough.

❯ ❯ ❯

MARZIPAN COOKIES WITH FIGS AND WALNUTS

To fill using a mold, start by dipping the mold into a bowl of flour, then gently press the dough circle into the mold. Place a teaspoon of walnut filling on each piece of dough. Fold the dough edges in to seal. Turn the mold over onto your work surface and press to seal. Remove the molded cookie from the mold.

To form a half-moon shape, place a rounded teaspoon of walnut filling in the center of each circle and fold in half to form a crescent shape. Press the edges with your fingers to seal. Place the cookies on the prepared baking sheet 2 inches apart. Refrigerate for at least 30 minutes, or up to overnight.

Preheat the oven to 325°F.

Bake the cookies until light golden brown, about 20 minutes. Cool completely on the baking sheet. Dust generously with confectioners' sugar. Store in an airtight container for up to 5 days.

These sesame bars are our best seller, by far. Lots of brown sugar combined with a thick, raw honey produce the caramel that holds the nuts and sesame seeds together over a thick shortbread crust. Cut them into small pieces; they are very rich and one or two bites is enough. Read the instructions carefully: the bars come out of the oven very underbaked and set up as they cool. Don't be tempted to bake them longer because the caramel will be too hard and not chewy. ◆ **MAURA**

MAKES 3 DOZEN

SESAME CASHEW BARS

Crust

2 cups plus 1 tablespoon all-purpose flour

1¾ sticks (7 ounces) unsalted butter, chilled and cut into ¼-inch cubes

⅔ cup firmly packed light brown sugar

½ teaspoon kosher salt

Filling

3½ cups salted cashews, coarsely chopped

2 tablespoons toasted sesame seeds (see page 241)

¼ teaspoon kosher salt

2 sticks (8 ounces) unsalted butter

¼ cup granulated sugar

1½ cups plus 2 tablespoons firmly packed light brown sugar

½ cup raw honey (see page 234)

5 tablespoons heavy cream

1 teaspoon vanilla extract

Line a 13 by 9-inch pan with aluminum foil, making sure it extends over the sides. Very lightly spray or butter the foil.

To make the crust, combine the flour, butter, brown sugar, and salt and in a food processor fitted with a metal blade. Pulse until the butter forms pieces the size of small pebbles, 20 to 30 seconds. Pour the crust crumbs into the prepared pan and press down to form an even layer. Cover and refrigerate for at least 30 minutes, or up to overnight.

Preheat the oven to 350°F.

Bake the crust until golden, about 25 minutes. Set aside to cool.

While the crust is cooling, make the filling. Combine the cashews, sesame seeds, and salt in a bowl. Mix well and set aside.

Melt the butter in a saucepan over low heat. Add the granulated and brown sugars and honey and cook over medium heat, whisking constantly, until the sugar dissolves and begins to turn to caramel, forming large bubbles and thickening, or reaches 240°F on a candy thermometer. Remove from the heat and whisk in the cream and vanilla. Using a rubber spatula, mix in the cashew mixture until well combined.

Pour the filling on top of the baked crust in an even layer. Return the pan to the oven and bake until the caramel bubbles along the sides of the pan only and the center is still liquid, 26 to 28 minutes. The filling will appear unbaked. It is very important not to overbake. The filling will set up as it cools.

Set aside to cool completely and then cover and refrigerate overnight.

Lift the foil out of the pan to remove the bars in one large block. Cut into thirty-six 1½-inch squares.

Store in an airtight container in the refrigerator for up to 2 weeks.

This is a very rich chocolate cookie, delicious on its own, but when combined with the halvah, it is a Sofra classic. I have been making a version of this cookie for my family and friends for years—I became known for them. So one year a good friend named them after me, and called them Maureos. I don't think our customers know that they are named after the pastry chef, but they have gotten used to the name. Halvah is a sesame confection made with tahini and sugar syrup. When it is baked, it becomes thick and caramelized; the combination of the deep caramel sesame and chocolate is like a peanut butter cup. The baked halvah is usually served as a dessert in Turkey. It is easy to make and can be served as pudding on its own with toasted pine nuts or with grape molasses. ♦ **MAURA**

MAKES ABOUT 18 SANDWICH COOKIES

MAUREOS WITH BAKED HALVAH

1½ cups plus 2 tablespoons all-purpose flour

6 tablespoons unsweetened cocoa powder

1 teaspoon baking soda

¼ teaspoon baking powder

½ teaspoon kosher salt

1¼ sticks (5 ounces) unsalted butter, chilled and cut into ¼-inch cubes

1½ cups sugar

1 egg

Baked Halvah

1 pound halvah (see page 234), crumbled

½ cup plus 2 tablespoons whole milk

2 tablespoons unsalted butter, softened

Lightly flour a work surface. Line a baking sheet with parchment paper.

Sift together the flour, cocoa powder, baking soda, baking powder, and salt. Set aside.

Combine the butter and sugar in the bowl of a stand mixer fitted with a paddle attachment. Start mixing on low speed to combine, then increase to medium speed and mix until light and fluffy, about 10 minutes. Scrape down the sides of the bowl. On low speed, add the egg and scrape the sides of the bowl again. Staying on low speed, add the flour mixture and mix until the dough is smooth.

Transfer the dough to the work surface. Divide the dough in half. Knead each piece until smooth. Roll each piece into a 12 by 10-inch rectangle with about a ¼-inch thickness. Using a pizza cutter or a knife, cut the dough into 1½-inch strips, then cut across the other side to make squares. Place each piece on the prepared baking sheet to chill. Gather the scraps to reroll and recut. Cover and refrigerate until firm, 1 hour. The cookies can also be prepared and frozen for up to 2 months. Defrost in the refrigerator for 2 hours or overnight before baking.

Preheat the oven to 350°F. Remove the cookies from the refrigerator and space them 2 inches apart on a baking sheet. Bake the cookies until the tops are crisp and cracked, 12 to 14 minutes. Set aside to cool on the baking sheet before filling.

To make the baked halvah, preheat the oven to 400°F. Butter an 8-inch baking dish. Place the crumbled halvah, milk, and butter in the bowl of a food processor. Process until smooth, with the consistency of hummus. Using a spatula, scrape the mixture into the prepared baking dish.

Bake for about 20 minutes, until set around the edges but still loose in the center. It should have turned a golden caramel color. Set aside to cool.

Scrape the halvah out of the pan into a small bowl. Stir until smooth, then refrigerate until ready to fill the cookies.

To fill the maureos, using a small spoon, place the baked halvah in the center of a baked cookies; place a second cookie on top, and press them together. Repeat with the remaining cookies.

Halawa, which means "sweet" in Arabic, refers to many different types of dense, sweet confections. Here, I am combining two of my favorite flavors: rose and mastic. I discovered how beautifully these flavors go together in Lebanon, where it is a popular combination that is somehow always perfectly balanced. The apricots are pressed into a bar and topped with white chocolate ganache. It is important to use a real white chocolate, such as Valrhona 35 percent Ivoire. You can keep it simple by omitting the ganache and instead dipping it in dark chocolate or tossing it in sesame seeds or confectioners' sugar. ◆ **MAURA**

MAKES 32 PIECES

APRICOT HALAWA WITH WHITE CHOCOLATE GANACHE

½ teaspoon ground mastic (see page 237)

1 pound dried apricots, chopped

2 teaspoons rose water (see page 241)

10 ounces white chocolate, chopped

¼ stick (1 ounce) unsalted butter

½ cup heavy cream

1 cup shelled toasted pistachios

Lightly spray an 8-inch square baking dish with nonstick cooking spray. Line with plastic wrap.

Grind the mastic pieces into a powder with a mortar and pestle.

Put the mastic and half the apricots in a food processor and process until a ball forms. Transfer to a bowl. Repeat with the remaining apricots. Add the rose water and mix by hand until you form a firm paste.

Press the mixture into the prepared pan in an even layer, using the bottom of a measuring cup to pack the apricots as firmly as possible. Cover and refrigerate for at least 30 minutes, or up to 1 week.

To make the ganache, put the white chocolate and butter in a bowl. Heat the heavy cream to just under a boil and pour into the bowl of chocolate. Set aside for 5 minutes, then stir with a rubber spatula until smooth. Chill the ganache until it starts to set around the edges but is still pourable, 30 minutes.

Pour the ganache over the chilled apricot layer. Cover and refrigerate until firm, at least 4 hours or up to 4 days.

Lift the plastic wrap to remove the halawa from the pan. Cut into 1-inch squares. Top each piece with a toasted pistachio. Store cut halawa in the refrigerator for 2 weeks. Bring to room temperature to serve.

WHITE CHOCOLATE White chocolate is not real chocolate; it consists of cocoa butter, sugar, and milk solids, but no cocoa solids, the main ingredient in chocolate. There are some imitation white chocolate morsels that contain palm oil, milk powder, and sugar. The ganache will not set up firmly using white chocolate morsels. It is important to use a real white chocolate like Valrhona, available at Whole Foods, or a white chocolate baking bar.

This is a traditional American cookie we offer at Sofra, and it is a favorite of the staff. I created this recipe for my dad, who loved sweets. These cookies have been a family favorite for years, and no family occasion is complete without them. Once mixed and chilled, they should be baked quickly or the oil will start to separate. ◆ **MAURA**

MAKES 2 DOZEN

MOLASSES COOKIES

2 cups all-purpose flour

2 teaspoons baking soda

½ teaspoon kosher salt

1 teaspoon ground cinnamon

½ teaspoon ground nutmeg

½ teaspoon ground cloves

¾ cup canola oil

¼ cup molasses

1¼ cups sugar

1 large egg

Combine the flour, soda, salt, cinnamon, nutmeg, and cloves in a bowl and set aside.

Combine the canola oil, molasses, 1 cup of the sugar, and the egg in the bowl of a stand mixer. Using a paddle attachment, mix on medium speed until the mixture is smooth and the oil is incorporated, about 30 seconds. Add the dry ingredients and mix on low speed until thoroughly combined and smooth.

Transfer the dough to a clean bowl, and cover and refrigerate until firm, about 2 hours, or up to overnight.

Preheat the oven to 350°F. Line a baking sheet with parchment paper. Put the remaining ¼ cup sugar in a bowl.

Using a tablespoon scoop, make small balls. Place the balls in the bowl of sugar, rolling to coat completely.

Place the balls on the prepared baking sheet ½ inch apart. Bake until the cookies are puffed and set around the edges but still appear underbaked, 12 to 14 minutes. Set aside to cool.

We serve these candied cashews on one of our most popular Oleana desserts, our brown butter profiteroles with sesame caramel sauce and halvah. These were created by Kate Henry, who was our pastry chef for five years at Oleana. The recipe is so addicting, I stole it for Sofra. These buttery, caramelized nuts are not only the perfect topping for ice cream; they're also an incredible snack on their own. They are one of Ana's favorites. ◆ **MAURA**

MAKES 4 CUPS

SESAME CARAMEL CASHEWS

3½ cups whole roasted cashews

1 cup toasted sesame seeds
(see page 241)

1½ teaspoons fleur de sel or
kosher salt

1 cup sugar

¼ cup water

2 tablespoons (1 ounce) unsalted
butter, at room temperature

Preheat the oven to 300°F. Line a baking sheet with parchment paper.

Spread the cashews on the prepared baking sheet and bake until warmed, 5 minutes. Combine the sesame seeds and fleur de sel; set aside.

Combine the sugar and water in a large shallow pan, like a roasting pan. This will make it easier to stir the nuts in a single layer to coat evenly. Cook over medium heat until the mixture turns to a medium caramel color, 5 minutes. Off the heat, add the warm cashews and stir quickly to coat with caramel. Stir in the butter and mix until evenly distributed. Add the sesame seeds and salt and stir until all the nuts are coated.

Pour onto the prepared baking sheet. Once the nuts have started to cool, break apart if they have clumped together. You can start snacking on them once they have cooled, or you can cover and store them in an airtight container at room temperature for up to 2 weeks.

SPECIALTY PASTRIES, CAKES, AND DESSERTS

The variety of pastries and cakes of the Middle East and Eastern Mediterranean is vast. The one thing they all have in common from culture to culture, kitchen to kitchen, is they are made with dedication and love. Yes, you could say that about all sweets, but Middle Eastern sweets are especially treasured because they are often associated with a religious ceremony or family tradition. They are usually eaten in the midafternoon with tea or offered to guests as they arrive at one's home. "Every meal without a sweet is an imperfection" is an Arabic saying, and as a pastry chef, Maura wholeheartedly agrees with giving sweets the attention and admiration shown by the Arabic traditions.

One constant feature of Middle Eastern desserts is the sugar syrup. Maura likes to use a lot of different flavors in her syrups, like spices or tea, as well as the traditional rose water or orange blossom water. Quantities of sugar and water can vary according to each dessert, but Maura generally sticks to a ratio of 1½ parts sugar to 1 part water and reduces it by keeping it at a low boil for 10 to 15 minutes. She has been told by Didem Hosgel, our Turkish chef, that she does not soak the pastries enough. This may be true for Didem, but we think Maura soaks it just the right amount for our Sofra patrons.

In this instance, we took a classic American recipe—pecan pie—and eased it into the Sofra repertoire by having some fun with ingredients, namely dates. The addition is simple— we added a layer of espresso-soaked dates to the bottom. They bring an unexpected, but pleasing, texture to the filling and help balance out the sweetness. ◆ **MAURA**

SERVES 6 TO 8

BROWN BUTTER PECAN PIE WITH ESPRESSO DATES

Pie Dough

1¼ cups all-purpose flour

½ teaspoon kosher salt

1½ teaspoons sugar

1 stick (4 ounces) unsalted butter, cut into ¼-inch cubes and frozen

¼ cup ice water

Espresso Dates

1 cup pitted and chopped Medjool dates, packed

3 tablespoons brewed espresso or strong coffee

Filling

2 cups pecans, coarsely chopped

1 stick (4 ounces) unsalted butter

1 cup firmly packed light brown sugar

1 cup Lyle's Golden Syrup or light corn syrup (see Cook's Note, page 169)

1½ teaspoons kosher salt

1½ teaspoons instant espresso

3 eggs

Lightly flour a work surface.

To make the pie dough, combine the flour, salt, sugar, and butter in the bowl of a stand mixer fitted with a paddle attachment. Mix on low speed until the dough resembles a very coarse mixture with large chunks of butter still visible. Add the ice water and mix on low speed until the dough is moistened but doesn't quite hold together.

Turn the crumbly mixture out onto the prepared work surface and finish working it together with your hands. Using the heel of your hand, "smear" the lumps of butter into the dough in long streaks, until most of the butter lumps are incorporated. Form the dough into a round disk, wrap it securely in plastic wrap, and refrigerate it for at least 6 hours, or up to 4 days, or freeze it for up to 2 months. If it is frozen, thaw it in the refrigerator overnight before using.

Remove the dough from the refrigerator and set aside at room temperature for 10 to 15 minutes to slightly soften. If it is stiff, knead a few times until smooth and pliable.

Generously flour a work surface. Using a rolling pin, roll the dough from the center of the circle up and away from you in a single direction; do not roll in a back-and-forth motion. Turn the dough as you roll to maintain a round shape; roll into a 12-inch circle. Drape the dough over the rolling pin and unroll it over the center of a 9-inch pie pan. Ease the dough into the pan and press the dough around the bottom and sides of the pan. There should be a 2-inch overlap around the edge of the pan; fold this excess dough in half, over the rim of the pan. Crimp the dough. Cover and freeze for at least 2 hours, or up to overnight.

Preheat the oven to 375°F.

Line the pie shell with parchment paper or aluminum foil and fill with pie weights (or dried beans). Bake the pie shell until the edges begin to brown, about 25 minutes. Remove the pie weights and return to the oven for 5 to 10 minutes to completely bake the center. Set aside to cool.

Lower the heat to 350°F.

To prepare the espresso dates, combine the dates and brewed espresso in a skillet. Keeping the dates in a single layer, cook over medium heat until the dates soften, 3 to 5 minutes. Remove from the heat and let cool. The liquid will be absorbed as it cools. The dates can be prepared up to 5 days in advance and refrigerated.

To make the filling, spread the chopped pecans in an even layer on a rimmed baking sheet. Place in the oven for about 8 minutes to lightly toast. Set aside to cool.

In a saucepan over medium heat, melt the butter and cook until it begins to brown and become fragrant, 3 to 4 minutes—be careful not to burn. Remove from the heat and set aside.

In a bowl, whisk together the brown sugar, golden syrup, salt, and instant espresso. Whisk in the eggs until smooth. Whisk in the browned butter.

Spread the espresso date mixture in an even layer on the bottom of the pie shell. Add the chopped pecans on top. Pour the egg mixture over the pecans.

Place the pie on the baking sheet and bake until the filling has risen and is set when you jiggle the pan, 50 to 60 minutes. Set aside to cool before serving.

COOK'S NOTE I prefer Lyle's Golden Syrup to light corn syrup. Lyle's is a full-flavored cane sugar syrup that lends a richer caramel flavor to pecan pie. It also improves the stability of the pie. It is available at many supermarkets in the baking aisle.

I once heard of a milk-soaked baklava, and I knew immediately I had to try to make my own. This is a lighter version of baklava, with the milk making the syrup less sugary and heavy. I decided to add soft, cooked figs, making the texture smooth and chewy rather than just crunchy from the walnuts. This has a very wintery flavor; the addition of orange and cloves makes it perfect for the holidays. The assembly is surprisingly easy; the phyllo is rolled into logs, so there is not a lot of layering involved. ◆ **MAURA**

MAKES 20 PIECES

MILKY WALNUT-FIG BAKLAVA

1 cup finely chopped dried black or white figs

¾ cup freshly squeezed orange juice

1½ cups toasted ground walnuts

½ teaspoon ground cloves

About 9 ounces/12 sheets phyllo (see Working with Phyllo, page 135)

6 ounces clarified butter (page 215)

1¼ cups whole milk

¾ cup sugar

To prepare the filling, combine the figs and orange juice in a small saucepan. Simmer over medium heat for 3 to 4 minutes until the figs plump up. Remove from the heat. Cool completely; the figs will absorb the juice as they cool. Add 1 cup of the walnuts and cloves and mix well.

Preheat the oven to 350°F. Butter an 8-inch square baking dish.

Place a sheet of parchment paper on a work surface. Lay the phyllo out right next to it. Place one sheet of phyllo on the parchment paper, with the shorter side facing you. Brush lightly with the clarified butter. Place another sheet on top of the first and butter it. Fold the phyllo in half down from the top so the shorter side is still facing you. Spread ½ cup of the filling in an even layer across the edge of the phyllo nearest you. Carefully roll the phyllo into a tight log. Hold each end of the log and squeeze together to make the log wrinkled. Place in the prepared baking dish; it should fit just perfectly. Repeat this process until you have four logs in the baking dish. Cut across the logs into 1-inch pieces. Bake until golden brown, 50 to 60 minutes.

While the baklava is baking, prepare the syrup. Combine the milk and sugar in a saucepan. Bring to a boil over medium heat, stirring to dissolve the sugar. Lower the heat to medium-low and simmer until thickened and reduced to 1 cup, about 15 minutes. Place in the refrigerator until the baklava is baked.

Remove the baklava from the oven and pour the chilled milk syrup over it. Set aside to cool and absorb the syrup. If you are not serving this right away, refrigerate it after it has cooled and the milk has been completely absorbed.

COOK'S NOTE Because of the milk, this baklava should be refrigerated and brought to room temperature before serving. Cut into small pieces and place each piece in a small cupcake paper liner with the open center facing up. For the filling, I prefer dried black mission figs.

This was originally created for the Oleana dessert menu and is now a signature Sofra item. I have added cacao nibs and cinnamon sticks to the syrup to impart a wonderful and slightly bitter edge to a very sweet dessert. Honey syrups are not usually used in Turkish baklava, but the combination of honey and the bittersweet chocolate was too appealing to pass up. ◆ **MAURA**

MAKES 24 SERVINGS

CHOCOLATE HAZELNUT BAKLAVA

Filling

1 pound whole blanched hazelnuts

12 ounces extra-bittersweet chocolate (70% cacao)

1½ tablespoons ground cinnamon

Syrup

2 cups water

1½ cups honey

1 cup sugar

½ cup cocoa nibs

2 cinnamon sticks

About 9 ounces/12 sheets phyllo (see Working with Phyllo, page 135)

12 ounces melted clarified butter (page 215)

Preheat the oven to 350°F.

To make the filling, spread out the hazelnuts on a rimmed baking sheet in a single layer. Bake until they are toasted, 12 to 15 minutes. Set aside to cool.

Using a food processor, pulse the hazelnuts until they are finely ground.

Chop the chocolate by hand or use the food processor. Pulse the chocolate to pieces similar in size to the hazelnuts. Combine the chocolate, hazelnuts, and cinnamon in a bowl.

To make the syrup, combine the water, honey, sugar, cocoa nibs, and cinnamon sticks in a saucepan and bring to a boil, stirring to dissolve the sugar. Lower the heat and keep at a low boil for 15 minutes. Set aside to cool. Strain; you should have 2½ cups. Preheat the oven to 350°F.

Cut the phyllo into 9 by 13-inch pieces. Generously butter the bottom and sides of 9 by 13-inch baking dish or a disposable aluminum baking pan.

Place one sheet of phyllo in the pan and butter the top. Repeat until you have eight sheets of phyllo for the bottom layer. Spread 2 cups of the filling evenly over the phyllo. Layer and butter four sheets of phyllo. Spread 2 cups of the filling in an even layer. Layer the four sheets of buttered phyllo on top. Spread the remaining filling over the phyllo. Butter and layer ten sheets of phyllo for the top layer Set aside at room temperature for 20 to 30 minutes; when the butter solidifies a bit, it will be easier to cut the baklava into pieces.

Using a ruler, cut into 3 by 3-inch squares; this will leave a small amount at one end. Cut each square diagonally into two triangles.

❯ ❯ ❯

CHOCOLATE HAZELNUT BAKLAVA

Place the pan on a baking sheet and bake for 25 minutes. Lower the temperature to 300°F and bake until golden brown and the top layers of phyllo appear separated, 45 to 50 minutes.

Pour or ladle the room-temperature syrup evenly over the hot baklava. Set aside to cool.

Remove the baklava by carefully sliding a thin spatula down and under the sides of the pan.

COOK'S NOTE It is best to build this baklava in a disposable 9 by 13-inch disposable aluminum baking pan. Then, when you remove the pieces of baklava, you can cut through the pan on one side, flatten that side, and slide a spatula in without losing any pieces. But it is necessary to not cut through the bottom of the pan when you precut the baklava or the syrup will leak out when it is soaked. The syrup can be made in advance and refrigerated for up to 4 days.

I love all types of custard desserts, so I was intrigued by this Greek one. Known as bougasta in Greece, it is the most popular breakfast treat, dusted with cinnamon and confectioners' sugar. But I think it makes a beautiful dessert, served warm with roasted apples or pears in the fall or fresh berries in the summer. It is a beautiful combination, with its crunchy exterior and creamy melt-in-the-mouth filling. The phyllo layer will actually bake lighter and flakier if you use very little butter on each sheet of phyllo. It is best served the day it is made. ◆ **MAURA**

MAKES 16 SERVINGS

MILK PIE

3 cups whole milk

Grated zest of 1 lemon

4 eggs

1 cup sugar

½ cup semolina flour

1 stick (4 ounces) unsalted butter, melted

About 4 ounces/6 sheets phyllo (see Working with Phyllo, page 135)

6 ounces clarified butter (page 215)

2 tablespoons confectioners' sugar

2 tablespoons ground cinnamon

Preheat the oven to 400°F. Butter an 8-inch square baking dish. Bring a pot of water to a boil to use as a water bath, reduce the heat, and keep at a simmer.

Combine the milk and lemon zest in a saucepan.

Combine the eggs and sugar in a bowl that is large enough to hold the milk. Whisk the eggs and sugar well, until smooth and pale, 2 minutes.

Bring the milk to a boil and quickly whisk in the semolina. Lower the heat and whisk continually until thickened, about 4 minutes. Pour into the egg mixture and whisk well to combine. Place the bowl over the simmering water. Whisk constantly over medium heat until very thick, gradually adding the melted butter. You can test it by seeing if lines remain in the top of the custard when the whisk goes across it.

Remove from the heat. Pour into a shallow container to cool. The filling can be prepared 2 days in advance and refrigerated.

Lay the phyllo out with the longer side facing you. Cut the phyllo in half down the center. Wrap half in plastic wrap for a future use. Using the square baking dish as a guide, cut the remaining piece of phyllo in half.

Place one sheet of phyllo into the buttered dish, lightly butter the sheet with clarified butter, and then place another sheet on top. Continue until you have eight buttered sheets. Spread the semolina filling in an even layer on top of the phyllo. Butter and layer 6 sheets of phyllo for the top layer. Butter the top sheet of phyllo with extra clarified butter.

≻ ≻ ≻

> > > **MILK PIE**

To portion, score the top layer only; do not cut through to the custard layer. Cut down the middle of the pie, then cut each half into two strips. Cut each of those four strips into four pieces, making sixteen 2-inch squares. Place the pan on a baking sheet. Bake until the top layer is light golden brown, 40 to 45 minutes. Set aside to cool.

Stir together confectioners' sugar and cinnamon and sprinkle over the top of the cooled pie. Serve at room temperature.

Also known as bulbul yavasi, or nightingale's nests, these have a hollow phyllo shell with a nut-filled center. Once filled with the nuts and soaked with syrup, the phyllo nest is a wonderful contrast of textures—the crunchy, soaked phyllo is surprisingly delicate with sweet syrup-soaked, sticky pistachios. This is a unique baklava that is great when you don't need to prepare a whole pan; you can make as many as you need. This recipe is easier than the directions will make it sound, believe me, and it always impresses. Read carefully first; it takes a lot of words to explain. You can purchase a ½-inch wooden dowel from the hardware store. ◆ **MAURA**

MAKES 8 PASTRIES

PISTACHIO BIRD'S NESTS

Lemon Syrup

1½ cups sugar

1 cup water

Juice and finely grated zest of 1 lemon

Nests

4 ounces clarified butter (page 215)

About 6 ounces/8 sheets phyllo (see Working with Phyllo, page 135)

1 cup toasted chopped pistachios

To prepare the lemon syrup, combine the sugar, water, lemon juice, and zest in a saucepan. Bring to a boil over medium-high heat to dissolve the sugar. Lower the heat to medium and keep at a low boil for 10 minutes until thickened.

Preheat the oven to 350°F.

To prepare the nests, lay the phyllo sheets on a work surface and cover with a clean towel. Place a sheet of parchment paper next to the phyllo to work on. Place a baking sheet, without parchment paper, next to the phyllo.

Place one sheet of phyllo on the parchment paper with the shorter side facing you. Lightly brush across the top, in the center, and across the bottom with clarified butter. If you use more butter than this, the wrinkles in the phyllo become less visible. Fold the edge of the phyllo closest to you up to within 1 inch of the top edge. Place the wooden dowel on the bottom folded edge, with the end of the dowel meeting the left end of the phyllo, and begin to loosely roll the phyllo around the dowel up to the unfolded edge. Lift the dowel and gently squish the phyllo to the left end. Slide it off the dowel, and form it into a circle with the reserved phyllo in the center, creating the center of the nest. Place on the baking sheet. Repeat with the remaining sheets of phyllo.

Bake until lightly golden, 15 minutes. Remove from the oven and fill the centers of each nest with chopped pistachios. Use a small measuring cup or ladle to soak each nest with ¼ cup of lemon syrup. Set aside to cool on the baking sheet.

Using a spatula, remove the nests from the pan. Serve at room temperature with some of the extra syrup from the baking sheet.

This is the easiest version of baklava, called a sarma, which means it is rolled. The best thing about this version of baklava is that it tastes like a phyllo-wrapped Butterfinger candy, with the tahini giving it a nut butter flavor! They're perfect when you don't need or want a full tray of baklava; just make as many as you need. I like using ground cashews, because they go so well with sesame, but any ground nut will work. Serve with vanilla ice cream and crumbled halvah. Or drizzle with melted chocolate to treat yourself to a Butterfinger. ◆ **MAURA**

MAKES 16 SERVINGS

SESAME CASHEW SARMA

1½ cups roasted, salted cashews

About 3 ounces/4 sheets phyllo (see Working with Phyllo, page 135)

4 ounces melted clarified butter (page 215)

½ cup tahini (see page 242)

¼ cup sugar

Confectioners' sugar for dusting

Preheat the oven to 350°F. Lightly butter an 8-inch square baking dish.

Finely grind the cashews in a food processor.

Lay the phyllo out on a work surface and place a dry towel on top. Place a sheet of parchment paper next to the phyllo to work on.

Place one sheet of phyllo onto the parchment paper, with the longer side facing you. Brush it lightly with butter. Place a second sheet on top. Brush it with tahini. If the tahini is too thick, microwave the tahini to loosen it up. It is easier to dab it on rather than brush an even layer. Sprinkle 2 tablespoons of sugar over the phyllo. Fold the phyllo in half left to right so you have the shorter side now facing you. Sprinkle ½ cup ground cashews over the surface. Roll into a tight log, starting at the shorter side. The log should be about 1½ inches around with the seam side down. Use a sharp knife to slice the log into 1½-inch pieces and place them into the prepared baking dish, cut side up, with sides touching. Repeat with the remaining phyllo. Brush a little butter across the tops. Sprinkle the remaining ground cashews evenly over the top.

Bake until golden brown, 18 to 20 minutes. Cool completely in the baking dish. Dust generously with confectioner's sugar.

Emily Weber, Sofra's pastry chef, brought this recipe to us. Her interest was piqued by the exotic-sounding name while searching for a special romantic dessert. Strangely, there is no special story behind the name. It's a lovely cake and surprisingly simple to prepare. We introduced it as a special dessert to take home on a Valentine's Day menu, and soon it became a fixture on our pastry counter. The spices come through in the moist and custardlike top layer, while the crumb crust stays sugary in the mouth, creating an amazing textural contrast. Serve with Greek yogurt and Rose Petal Jam (page 226) on the side for another tangy contrast. ◆ **MAURA**

SERVES 8 TO 10

PERSIAN LOVE CAKE

3 cups almond flour (see page 231)

1 cup granulated sugar

1 cup firmly packed light brown sugar

½ teaspoon kosher salt

1 stick (4 ounces) unsalted butter, at room temperature

2 eggs, lightly beaten

1 cup plus 1 tablespoon plain whole-milk Greek yogurt, plus more to serve

1 tablespoon Persian Spice (page 218)

1 teaspoon rose water

½ cup honey

½ cup sliced natural (skin-on) almonds

Preheat the oven to 350°F. Butter a 9-inch springform pan or spray with nonstick cooking spray.

Combine the almond flour, granulated sugar, brown sugar, and salt in a bowl. Add the butter with your hands and mix until it forms a coarse crumb texture. Spoon half the crumb mixture into the prepared pan, pressing down to form a crust. Set aside.

Add the eggs, yogurt, Persian Spice, and rose water to the remaining crumb mixture and mix with a rubber spatula until smooth and creamy. Spread in an even layer over the crumb crust.

Bake until golden brown and slightly puffed in the center, 30 to 35 minutes.

Meanwhile, spread the almonds on a baking sheet and toast them in the oven with the cake for 12 minutes. Set aside.

Brush the top of the cake with honey while it is warm. Arrange toasted almonds around the edges.

Set aside to cool before removing from pan.

Serve with a spoonful of Greek yogurt.

This is one of Sofra's most popular cakes and one of my personal favorites. The rose water is very subtle, which is important because too much will make the cake bitter. Be sure to use a good-quality rose water, such as Mymouné brand (page 241). At Sofra, we serve this cake dolloped with our own Rose Petal Jam (page 226). It can also be used as a layer cake with lemon buttercream, perfect in the summer accompanied by peaches and seasonal berries. ◆ **MAURA**

MAKES 8 SERVINGS

ALMOND ROSE CAKE

1 cup all-purpose flour

1½ teaspoons baking powder

¼ teaspoon kosher salt

6 eggs

2 teaspoons rose water

8 ounces almond paste (see page 231), broken into ¼-inch pieces

1¼ cups sugar

2¼ sticks (9 ounces) unsalted butter, at room temperature

Rose Petal Jam (page 226), to serve

Preheat the oven to 325°F. Butter and lightly flour a 9-inch round cake pan.

Put the flour, baking powder, and salt in a bowl and combine with a whisk.

Put the eggs and rose water in a separate bowl. Do not combine.

Put the almond paste and sugar in the bowl of a stand mixer fitted with a paddle attachment and beat on low speed until the almond paste is similar in texture to the sugar crystals. Add the butter, a little bit at a time, and beat until well incorporated, about 2 minutes. Turn off the machine and scrape down the sides of the bowl.

Increase the speed to medium and beat until light and fluffy, 3 to 5 minutes. Scrape down the sides of the bowl. Decrease the speed to low, add the eggs with rose water, one egg at a time, and beat until they are fully incorporated, about 1 minute. Scrape down the sides of the bowl. Add the dry ingredients and mix until just combined.

Pour the batter in an even layer into the prepared cake pan. Bake until the center springs back when touched, 1 to 1¼ hours. Set aside to cool in the pan.

Serve at room temperature with Rose Petal Jam.

ROSE WATER For years, although I didn't love either, I used rose water and orange blossom water because I was "supposed to." All that changed on a trip to Lebanon, where I discovered Mymouné, products that are made by Lebanese sisters Youmna Goraieb and Leila Maalouf at the foot of Lebanon's Mount Sannine. Mymouné rose water is made in May, when the roses bloom; the rose water is the distilled essence of those rose petals.

Mymouné is known for using pure ingredients and producing small batches. Their rose water is so beautiful and worth every cent. When I got home from Lebanon, I immediately dumped all the cheap rose water down the drain, and now, there is no substitute in my mind.

Umm Ali translates as "Ali's mother." It is an Egyptian bread pudding using toasted phyllo. It is easy to make, and you can change the filling to any fruit and nut combination. The texture is surprising because it is not a custard-based pudding; it is the starch of the phyllo that holds it together. After preparing the toasted phyllo flakes, it is easy to assemble and bake. Use peaches and pistachios in the summer or keep it real simple and open a jar of marmalade; the mixture is entirely up to your tastes. The phyllo combines with the cream for the bread-pudding texture and, combined with the crunchy nuts and sweet fruit, this makes a great breakfast, served warm with chilled cream poured on top, like a bowl of cereal. ◆ **MAURA**

SERVES 6 TO 8

UMM ALI WITH CARAMELIZED APPLES

½ cup sliced natural (skin-on) almonds

About 8 ounces/12 sheets phyllo (see Working with Phyllo, page 135)

2½ sticks (10 ounces) unsalted butter

1 cup golden raisins

1¼ cups plus 2 tablespoons sugar

4 apples, peeled, cored, and cut into ¼-inch pieces

1½ cups whole milk

1½ cups heavy cream, plus more, chilled, to serve

1 teaspoon ground cinnamon

Preheat the oven to 350°F. Line a baking sheet with parchment paper. Lay a sheet of parchment paper on a work surface.

Spread out the almonds on a rimmed baking sheet and toast for 8 minutes. Set aside to cool.

Lay the sheets of phyllo next to the parchment paper. Melt 2 sticks of the butter and lightly brush each sheet of phyllo; it is not necessary to brush each sheet thoroughly. Scrunch each piece of the phyllo into a mound and place on the prepared baking sheet.

Bake until light golden and crisp, 15 to 20 minutes. Set aside to cool.

Crumble the phyllo with your hands into small cereal-like flakes. If some pieces are not crisp, place them back on the baking sheet and toast for a few minutes. Cover and refrigerate up to 1 week in an airtight container.

Put the raisins in a small bowl and cover with warm water. Drain and set aside.

Melt the remaining ½ stick butter in a skillet. Add ¾ cup of the sugar and stir until the sugar dissolves and begins to caramelize around the edges, about 5 minutes.

Add the apples, lower the heat, and cook until the sugar is melted and the apples are soft when pierced with a knife, 4 minutes. Add the raisins and cook for 1 minute. Set aside to cool.

Preheat the oven to 400°F. Butter an 8-inch square baking dish.

To assemble the pudding, combine the milk, cream, and ½ cup of the sugar in a saucepan over medium heat, stirring just to dissolve the sugar. Set aside to cool.

Spread 2 cups phyllo flakes in an even layer in the prepared baking dish. Top with a layer of almonds, then the apple mixture. Top with the remaining phyllo flakes, reserving ½ cup. Pour the cream mixture into the pan. Add the reserved phyllo flakes if there are any gaps on top. Combine the cinnamon and remaining 2 tablespoons of sugar; sprinkle over the top.

Place the dish on a baking sheet. Bake until the cream starts to bubble up the sides and the top is toasted, 15 to 20 minutes. Scoop the pudding out into bowls and serve warm with chilled cream poured over it.

This recipe was a real team effort among the baking staff. Although the addition of the stout is clearly not an Arabic twist, we agreed it was our favorite version of this dish. We prefer a stout with some bitterness, like chicory. ◆ **MAURA**

MAKES 24 PIECES

SOFRA'S GINGERBREAD

Bread

1 cup stout, preferably chicory or oatmeal

1⅓ cups molasses

¼ cup plus 1 tablespoon brewed coffee

1½ teaspoons baking soda

2½ cups all-purpose flour

2½ tablespoons cocoa powder

2 teaspoons baking powder

¼ cup ground ginger

2 teaspoons ground cinnamon

1 teaspoon ground nutmeg

1 teaspoon kosher salt

¼ cup raw sugar

1 cup sugar

4 large eggs

1 cup canola oil

Glaze

1½ cups confectioners' sugar

¼ cup cocoa powder

½ cup brewed coffee

Cacao nibs (for garnish, optional)

In a large saucepan, combine the stout, molasses, and coffee. Bring to a boil, whisking to combine. Take the pan off the heat, and quickly whisk in the baking soda. The mixture will rise rapidly in the pot. Set aside until cooled and bubbles have subsided.

Preheat the oven to 350°F. Butter a 13 by 9-inch baking dish and line it with parchment paper.

Sift together the flour, cocoa powder, baking powder, ginger, cinnamon, nutmeg, and salt.

Combine the sugars in a separate bowl.

Using a stand mixer fitted with a whisk attachment, whisk the eggs on medium, slowly adding the sugars. Increase to high and whisk until pale and tripled in volume, about 7 minutes. Lower the speed and slowly pour in the canola oil and whisk another minute. Add the cooled stout mixture and whip until fully combined. Add the flour, increase the speed to medium, and beat until smooth, about 1 minute.

Pour the batter into the prepared pan. Bake until a toothpick inserted in the center comes out clean, 35 to 40 minutes.

To make the glaze, combine the confectioner's sugar and cocoa powder in a bowl. Whisk in the coffee until smooth.

Once the cake is cooled, spread an even layer of the glaze over the top of the cake. Cut into 2-inch pieces and top each piece with cacao nibs. The cake will keep at room temperature for 4 days.

Sometimes spelled k'nafe or kanafeh, kunefe is two layers of crunchy, golden kataifi (shredded phyllo), filled with cheese and soaked in sugar syrup. Popular versions are in every country in the Middle East. In Turkey it comes from the southern region, where it is made with a special cheese and baked to order at most restaurants. This version is a perfect example of how I read and test dozens of recipes before putting all that I like together in one of my own. In Lebanon, they used bread crumbs instead of phyllo, so I decided to combine them with the shredded phyllo to add a little crunch. After testing many fillings and different cheeses, I stopped with this one, for now. The mildness of mozzarella combined with how the milk pudding sets up is beautiful. ◆ **MAURA**

SERVES 8 TO 10

KUNEFE

8 ounces kataifi pastry (see page 236) or shredded phyllo

1 cup panko bread crumbs

1 stick (4 ounces) unsalted butter, melted

2 cups whole milk

¼ cup semolina flour

2 cups shredded mozzarella (best to purchase already shredded cheese)

1½ cups water

2 cups sugar

4 whole cloves

2 star anise

Preheat the oven to 350°F. Butter an 8-inch square baking dish.

To prepare the kataifi, put the kataifi in a medium bowl. Separate the strands with your hands, breaking into roughly 1-inch threads. Add the panko and melted butter. Toss with your hands, coating all the strands.

Put half of the kataifi mixture in the prepared baking dish. Bake until lightly golden brown, 20 minutes. Cover the remaining kataifi with plastic wrap until you are ready to finish.

To prepare the cheese filling, bring the milk to a boil over medium heat in a saucepan. Quickly whisk in the semolina, lower the heat, and continue whisking until the milk is thickened, about 3 minutes. Look for large bubbles to appear on the surface of the milk. Add the mozzarella; whisk until it melts.

Pour the cheese mixture on the kataifi in an even layer, spreading out into the corners. Arrange the remaining kataifi on top in a loose layer. Place the baking dish on a baking sheet. Bake until golden brown on top, 40 to 50 minutes.

While it is baking, prepare the spiced syrup. Combine the water, sugar, cloves, and star anise in a saucepan. Bring to a boil over medium heat, stirring to dissolve the sugar. Lower the heat and cook until the syrup starts to thicken, about 15 minutes. Strain and discard the spices.

Pour 1½ cups of the spiced syrup over the hot kataifi.

This dish is best served warm. Cut into 8 to 10 pieces and serve with the remaining spiced syrup alongside.

When the beautiful produce starts to arrive from Siena Farms, I imagine what I can do with it other than make savory pastries. This cake is the perfect embodiment of our farm-to-bakery connection. It will be bright red as it goes into the oven but it bakes to a dark chocolate color. Beets add moisture and depth—as well as sweetness—to a chocolate cake, but impart no beet flavor. ◆ **MAURA**

SERVES 8 TO 10

CHOCOLATE BEET CAKE

Cake

1½ pounds beets

2 ounces bittersweet chocolate (70% cacao)

1¼ cups all-purpose flour

¼ cup unsweetened cocoa powder

1 teaspoon baking soda

1 teaspoon kosher salt

2 eggs

1 cup sugar

¾ cup plus 2 tablespoons canola oil

Olive Oil Glaze

1½ cups confectioners' sugar

3 to 4 tablespoons whole milk

3 tablespoons extra-virgin olive oil, plus more as needed

Preheat the oven to 400°F.

To prepare the beets, put the beets in a small pan and cover with foil. Bake until tender when pierced with a knife, about 1 hour. Once they have cooled, peel them and remove the stems and roots. Chop into small pieces and then place in a food processor and process until the mixture becomes a coarse puree; you should have 1 cup. Set aside. Cover and refrigerate for up to 3 days.

Preheat the oven to 350°F. Butter an 8-inch round cake pan. Cover the bottom with a parchment-paper circle.

Melt the chocolate in a small bowl over a pot of simmering water, 3 to 4 minutes. Set aside to cool.

Sift together the flour, cocoa powder, baking soda, and salt. Set aside.

Put the eggs in the bowl of a stand mixer fitted with a whisk attachment and beat on medium speed, slowly adding the sugar, until the mixture is thick and pale, 4 to 5 minutes. Lower the speed and slowly pour in the canola oil. Add the melted chocolate and scrape the sides of the bowl.

Add the flour mixture and mix on low speed until almost combined. Add the beets and mix until well combined. Finish folding with a rubber spatula until the batter is smooth.

Pour into the prepared pan and bake until a toothpick inserted in the center comes out clean, 40 to 45 minutes. Set aside to cool completely in the pan.

To prepare the glaze, combine the confectioners' sugar, milk, and olive oil in a bowl. Whisk until smooth. If you need to thin it out a bit, add more olive oil instead of milk for flavor.

Remove the cake from the pan and place on a serving platter. Spread the glaze evenly over the top. Serve at room temperature.

This syrup-soaked semolina sponge cake is known as revani in Turkey and Greece, but other Middle Eastern countries have similar versions. This cake is a lovely dessert, but I also love it served with fruit and yogurt as breakfast. ◆ **MAURA**

MAKES 8 PIECES

REVANI (SYRUP-SOAKED SEMOLINA CAKE)

2 cups all-purpose flour

1 cup semolina flour

1 tablespoon baking powder

½ teaspoon baking soda

½ teaspoon kosher salt

1 cup plain whole-milk Greek yogurt, plus more to serve

Grated zest of 2 lemons

1 tablespoon vanilla extract

3 eggs, at room temperature

½ cup sugar

1 cup canola oil

1 cup toasted and finely chopped pistachios, to serve

Chamomile Syrup

1½ cups water

1 tablespoon loose chamomile tea

2 cups sugar

1 tablespoon freshly squeezed lemon juice

Preheat the oven to 350°F. Butter an 8-inch square baking dish.

Put the flours, baking powder, baking soda, and salt in a bowl and whisk to combine. Set aside.

Combine the yogurt, lemon zest, and vanilla in another bowl. Set aside.

Combine the eggs and sugar in the bowl of a stand mixer fitted with a whisk attachment. Whip on medium speed until pale yellow and tripled in volume, about 5 minutes. Lower the speed to low and slowly pour in the canola oil. Add the yogurt mixture in two additions. Scrape down the sides of the bowl. Add the dry ingredients and mix until just combined. Fold by hand with a rubber spatula until the batter is smooth.

Pour the batter into the prepared pan. Bake until a toothpick inserted in the center comes out clean, 35 to 40 minutes.

Prepare the syrup while the cake is baking. Bring the water to a boil in a small saucepan. Remove from the heat, add the tea leaves, cover, and let steep for 5 minutes.

Strain and discard the tea leaves. Return the liquid to the saucepan and add the sugar and lemon juice; bring to a boil. Lower the heat and simmer for 8 minutes, until reduced to 1¼ cups.

As soon as the cake is out of the oven, pour the hot chamomile syrup evenly over the cake. Set the cake aside to absorb the syrup completely while it cools. Invert the cake onto a platter to hold the syrup.

Slice and serve with a spoonful of yogurt and chopped pistachios.

This is the only filled and frosted cake we make at Sofra. It is made for our business partner, Gary Griffin, any time he wants it, and we sell it every Easter. The caramel sauce for the frosting has halvah in it (and halvah is grated over the top as well). Halvah is a sesame paste candy, available at many Middle Eastern grocery stores. Our recipe makes two cups of sauce, and since the recipe requires only one, try adding the remaining sauce to coffee or drizzling it on ice cream.

 This caramel sauce was originally developed for our Turkish-style profiteroles at Oleana. The magic comes from the addition of the halvah. While it's an extra step, it's well worth it because of the surprising combination of carrot and sesame. ◆ **MAURA**

SERVES 8

CARROT CAKE WITH SESAME CARAMEL CREAM CHEESE

Sesame Caramel Sauce

1½ cups sugar

¼ cup water

¾ stick (3 ounces) unsalted butter, at room temperature

1½ ounces halvah, crumbled

¾ cup heavy cream

1 teaspoon kosher salt

Carrot Cake

2 cups all-purpose flour

1 teaspoon kosher salt

2 teaspoons baking soda

1 tablespoon ground cinnamon

1 teaspoon ground allspice

2 tablespoons toasted sesame seeds (optional) (see page 241)

1 cup sweetened shredded coconut

4 eggs, at room temperature

2 cups sugar

1 cup canola oil

4 cups grated carrots

To make the sesame caramel sauce, combine the sugar and water in a small saucepan over medium heat and cook until the sugar dissolves and the mixture begins to boil, about 3 minutes. Once the mixture is boiling, do not stir. Cook until the sugar turns pale golden, about 8 minutes. If the caramel is cooked too far, the sesame flavor disappears.

Remove from the heat and add the butter, halvah, cream, and salt, one at a time; whisk until the halvah dissolves. Set aside to cool. Cover and refrigerate for up to 4 weeks.

Preheat the oven to 350°F. Butter and lightly flour two 9-inch round cake pans.

To make the carrot cake, put the flour, salt, baking soda, cinnamon, allspice, sesame seeds, and coconut in a large bowl and mix to combine. Set aside.

Put the eggs and sugar in the bowl of a stand mixer fitted with a paddle attachment and beat on medium speed until thickened and pale, 6 to 8 minutes.

Lower the speed to low and slowly add the oil in a steady stream. Scrape down the sides of the bowl. Add the flour mixture and mix until thoroughly combined. Fold in the carrots by hand.

Divide the batter evenly between the two prepared pans. Bake until a skewer inserted in the center comes out clean, 35 to 45 minutes. Set aside to cool in the pans.

Frosting

1 pound cream cheese,
at room temperature

1 cup Sesame Caramel
Sauce, cold

½ stick (2 ounces) unsalted
butter, at room temperature

4 to 5 ounces halvah, grated,
(see page 234)

To make the frosting, put the cream cheese in the bowl of a stand mixer fitted with a paddle attachment and mix on medium speed until it is completely smooth, 2 to 3 minutes. Add the caramel sauce and mix until well blended. Add 2 tablespoons of the butter and mix until completely smooth. Add the remaining 2 tablespoons of butter and mix again until completely smooth.

To frost the cake, place one cake layer in the center of a serving plate or cake stand. Spoon about ½ cup frosting onto the center of the cake. Using a spatula, spread the frosting evenly around the cake until it reaches the edges. Add more frosting as needed to create a layer about ¼ inch thick. Place the second cake layer on top. Spoon about 1 cup of the remaining frosting onto the center of the cake. Spread the frosting evenly around the cake until it reaches the edges, adding more frosting as needed. Smooth the frosting out from the center, letting it build up along the edges of the cake. Use the extra frosting at the edges of the cake and whatever frosting is left over to frost the sides. Sprinkle with the grated halvah and serve.

A financier is a small French cake made with almond meal and brown butter. I thought tahini would go beautifully with those flavors. These individual cakes are characterized by their crunchy exterior and moist interior. I use standard muffin pans for these petite cakes and add the extra crunch of sesame seeds and ground cacao nibs, finishing with a brush of bold honey on the top. ◆ **MAURA**

MAKES 18 CAKES

SESAME FINANCIERS

2 sticks plus 1 tablespoon (8½ ounces) unsalted butter

½ cup tahini (see page 242)

⅔ cup all-purpose flour

1 cup almond flour (see page 231)

2 cups confectioners' sugar

1 teaspoon kosher salt

8 ounces egg whites (approximately 7 egg whites)

2 tablespoons cacao nibs, pulsed in a spice grinder into coarse, small pieces

2 tablespoons toasted sesame seeds (see page 241)

Chestnut honey for brushing the tops

Sesame Caramel Cashews (page 165)

To prepare the brown butter, put the butter in a small saucepan and cook over medium heat until it is medium brown, 3 to 5 minutes. There is not much butter, so this will turn quickly. Remove from the heat. Stir in the tahini.

Preheat the oven to 325°F. Butter 18 holes in two standard muffin pans or spray with nonstick cooking spray.

Combine the flour, almond flour, confectioners' sugar, and salt in a medium bowl. Whisk to combine. Pour in egg whites and browned butter mixture, whisking by hand until smooth. Scoop 2 tablespoons of batter into each muffin cup. Lightly sprinkle the crushed cacao nibs and sesame seeds on top.

Bake until brown around the sides and the tops spring back when you touch them, 20 to 22 minutes.

Remove from the oven and brush the tops with the honey immediately. Cool in pans. Serve at room temperature with Sesame Caramel Cashews.

BEVERAGES

The Sofra counter staff and managers are responsible for producing a variety of house-made beverages. Every morning, they prepare their "drinkventory," a master sheet for beverages, pastry glazes, and syrups. They work on a small table right in front of the espresso machine, steps away from the kitchen crew. They are part of our production team, taking pride in producing unique Sofra beverages and hospitality.

We did not start off with such an ambitious house-made beverage program. But the popularity of our own chai blend and Lada's iced tea inspired us to keep creating and to get the counter staff involved in the process, encouraging them to come up with creations of their own. These drinks complete the Sofra experience of abundance and enjoyment.

The staff usually has time to begin their larger drink projects in the late afternoon, sometimes starting with cutting a tub of lemons and sugar to sit overnight, sometimes brewing a container of Blue Flower Earl Grey to rest overnight before the chai syrup is bottled and labeled with a date. It has been fun for all of us to see this grow into such a collaboration of kitchen and front-of-house staff, truly demonstrating the teamwork that defines Sofra.

Instead of juicing lemons, we remove the peel and pith and keep the lemons intact to produce a tart but balanced lemonade. Start this recipe one day before serving; we macerate the lemons and sugar overnight. ◆ **MAURA**

MAKES 1½ QUARTS

ORANGE BLOSSOM LEMONADE

1½ pounds lemons
(5 to 6 lemons)

¾ cup sugar

3 cups water

1 teaspoon orange blossom water

Fresh spearmint leaves

To prepare the lemons, cut the tip off at one end. Starting at the open end of the lemon, cut strips down the sides to remove the peel and white pith. Cut the lemons in half and put in a bowl. Add the sugar and toss well. Cover and refrigerate overnight.

Pour half the lemon mixture, including the liquid, into a blender and puree until smooth. Pour into a bowl; repeat with remaining lemon mixture. Add the water and stir to combine.

Using a fine-mesh strainer, strain the lemonade. Taste for sweetness and add more sugar, if needed. Add the orange blossom water.

To serve, pour over ice and garnish with fresh mint.

Lada Snikeris worked as a server at Oleana, Sofra's sister restaurant, from 2001 to 2008. This was her "secret" recipe that she made the kitchen staff every hot summer night before service. I always looked forward to a glass of this slightly savory, icy beverage that helped enable our night's work. It is now on the menu. This brew, inspired by the wild herbs and blossoms that grow around the great Lake Sevan in Armenia, contains linden flowers, elderberries, mint, and rosehips, with nettles for a light, savory, vegetal taste. You can make this recipe substituting your favorite herbal tea blend, or combine equal amounts of mint and black tea to concoct a caffeinated version. ◆ **ANA**

MAKES 1½ QUARTS

LADA'S ICED TEA

3 tablespoons loose Sevan blend tea or other loose herbal tea, such as spearmint

8 cups just-boiled water

¼ cup orange marmalade

½ cup apricot jam

½ cup freshly squeezed orange juice

2 tablespoons freshly squeezed lemon juice

6 cups ice

To steep the tea, put the tea in a stainless steel pot or deep mixing bowl. Add the hot water, cover, and set aside for 8 to 10 minutes. The tea should be pale and transparent.

Strain the tea through a fine-mesh sieve into a glass or ceramic pitcher large enough to hold a half gallon. Set aside to cool to room temperature.

Add the orange marmalade, apricot jam, orange juice, and lemon juice. Blend with an immersion blender or in a blender. Strain again.

Pour over ice and serve.

This refreshing iced tea is one of our most popular beverages. When brewing green tea, it is important not to oversteep it. An overly long steeping time will result in more bitterness and the loss of the delicate flavor green tea has. We use Turkish Cherry Nectar from Tamek, but you can use any cherry juice, which is available at Whole Foods or Trader Joe's. When fresh cherries aren't in season, you can also use frozen cherries to intensify the flavor. ◆ **MAURA**

RED DRAGON ICED TEA

2 teaspoons loose green tea

2½ cups just-boiled water

½ cup sugar

1 cup pitted Bing cherries

4 cups cherry nectar

1 tablespoon freshly squeezed lemon juice

To steep the tea, put the tea in a stainless steel pot or deep mixing bowl. Add 2 cups of the hot water, cover, and set aside for 5 minutes. Strain into a pitcher and set aside.

To make the cherry syrup, combine the sugar and the remaining ½ cup hot water in a small saucepan. Bring to a boil, stirring to dissolve the sugar. Add the cherries and boil until the cherries have softened, about 5 minutes.

Use an immersion blender to puree the cherries in the saucepan or put the mixture in a blender and puree until smooth. Strain into the pitcher with the brewed tea.

Cover and set aside to cool to room temperature.

Serve over ice.

As a nod to our love of spices and spice blends, we created our own unique chai blend. Rather than infusing spices into milk or tea, we create a sweet chai syrup for a much more concentrated flavor. This way you can keep the syrup in the refrigerator and prepare a single cup at any time. ◆ **MAURA**

MAKES 1½ CUPS OF SYRUP FOR 2 QUARTS OF TEA

SOFRA'S CHAI TEA

Chai Syrup

2 teaspoons whole black peppercorns

4 whole green cardamom pods

2 cinnamon sticks

½ teaspoon ground nutmeg

½ teaspoon ground ginger

1 tablespoon grated lemon zest (from about 1 lemon)

2 cups water

1 cup sugar

Tiny pinch of saffron

¼ cup loose black tea, such as Earl Grey

3 cups just-boiled water

4 cups whole or low-fat milk

To make the chai syrup, put the peppercorns and cardamom pods in a small plastic bag. Using a rolling pin, crush and crack them open. Combine the peppercorns, cardamom, cinnamon sticks, nutmeg, ginger, and lemon zest in a saucepan. Add the water and sugar. Bring the mixture to a boil, stirring to dissolve the sugar. Lower the heat and simmer until the syrup is reduced by half, about 20 minutes. Set aside to cool.

Once the syrup has cooled, stir in the saffron. Transfer to a small container and refrigerate overnight.

To brew the tea, put the tea in a stainless steel pot or deep mixing bowl. Add the hot water, cover, and set aside 6 to 8 minutes. The tea will be dark but not cloudy. Strain and set aside.

To prepare the chai tea, strain the chai syrup. Combine it with the brewed tea. Cover and refrigerate for up to 4 days.

To make warm chai, add the milk to the chai base in a saucepan. Heat over medium heat until the mixture just starts to boil. Remove from the heat and serve.

To make iced chai, add the milk to the chai base. Pour over ice and serve.

To make individual cups of chai, combine ⅔ cup chai syrup to ⅓ cup milk, then follow the directions above for making warm or iced chai.

You know you're obsessed with tahini when the thought of drinking it seems a perfect idea. This is a very rich treat, best served in small cups with sesame seeds and a touch of flaky salt on top. Use a combination of bittersweet and smooth milk chocolate for the perfect texture and richness. This little cup is an indulgence, so find a good-quality chocolate brand, such as Valrhona, and choose a bittersweet chocolate with 70 percent cacao. ◆ **MAURA**

MAKES 1½ QUARTS

TAHINI HOT CHOCOLATE

8 ounces milk chocolate, chopped

8 ounces bittersweet chocolate (70 percent cacao), chopped

4½ cups whole milk

½ cup tahini (see page 241)

1½ teaspoons kosher salt

¼ cup toasted sesame seeds (see page 242)

Fleur de sel

Combine the chocolates in a bowl and set aside.

Combine the milk and tahini in a saucepan over medium heat. Bring to just under a boil, whisking to incorporate the tahini.

Pour the milk mixture into the bowl of chocolate and set aside for 3 to 5 minutes, until the chocolate is almost melted. Stir with a rubber spatula until the chocolates all melt. Once the mixture is smooth, whisk vigorously or use an immersion blender to blend until smooth. Add the salt.

To serve, pour into small serving cups and top with toasted sesame seeds and a pinch of fleur de sel.

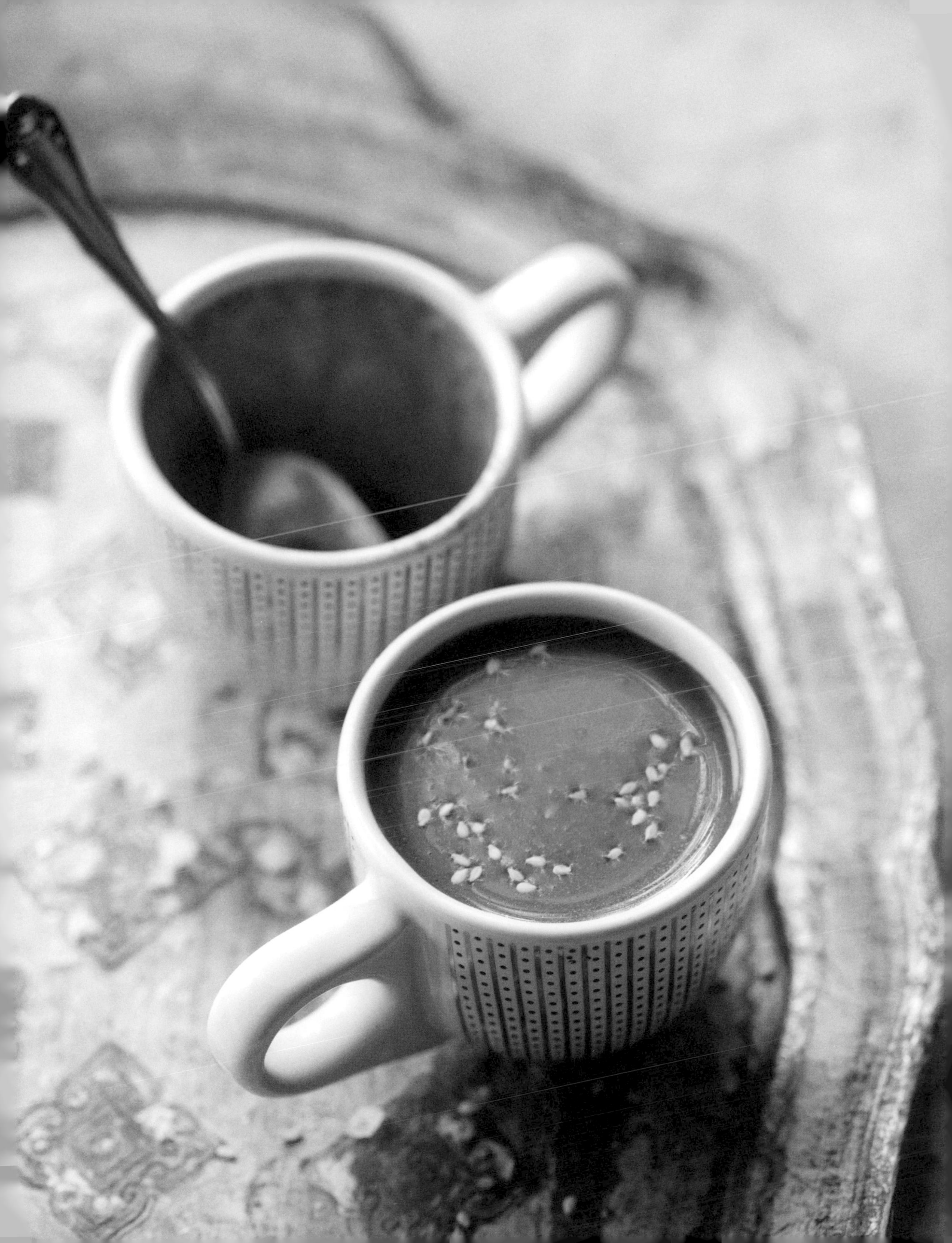

PANTRY

If we had to narrow down our condiments, spice blends, jams, pickles, and nut toppings to just a dozen, these would be the ones. Here lie the building blocks, the heart and soul, of many dishes and pastries at Sofra. We always have these on hand, and they are used frequently, transforming simple recipes into something special.

When you have condiments like these at home, you can renew an ordinary roasted chicken with toum, boost a burger on the fly with zhoug, or adorn a vegetarian chili with baharat. A small handful of za'atar almonds spooned over creamy hummus, whipped lentils, or thick yogurt can take the humdrum out of a quick meal.

Homemade is happiness, and the Middle Eastern pantry is stocked with sauces, preserves, and condiments to capture the bounty of a season and pack away vivid flavors to have on hand.

Pickles are so popular in the Middle East that there are stores and street vendors dedicated to them. A passerby can stop for a quick pickle snack and, in the hot weather, the pickle juice is often drunk to quench thirst. Whether pickles are served with grilled meats or falafel, their acidity cuts through richness and helps digestion.

White turnip pickles, or torshi in Turkish, are a favorite and are traditionally colored light or bright pink by adding a slice of beet to the brine. My favorite turnip is the hakurei, a Japanese variety that is small, crisp, and so sweet that I mostly enjoy them raw. They make an excellent salad turnip and a great quick pickle. ◆ **ANA**

MAKES 8 CUPS

PICKLED HAKUREI TURNIPS

2 pounds hakurei turnips

8 cups water

½ cup kosher salt

1 cup white wine vinegar

½ cup whole garlic cloves, smashed and peeled

2 bay leaves

1 tablespoon brown mustard seeds

1 tablespoon coriander seeds

2 tablespoons black peppercorns

1 large bunch fresh thyme, coarsely chopped

2 (½-inch) slices red beet (don't need to peel)

Trim the tops and bottoms of the turnips so that they are clean and sit on the cutting board without rolling around. Cut them into ½-inch wedges.

In a large saucepan over high heat, combine the water with the salt, vinegar, garlic, bay leaves, mustard seeds, coriander seeds, peppercorns, thyme, and beet slices. Bring to a boil. Lower the heat and simmer for 5 minutes.

Put the turnips in a nonreactive glass or stainless steel bowl and pour the simmering brine over them. Cover the bowl with a clean kitchen towel and leave at room temperature for 3 hours. Refrigerate the pickles at least overnight, or up to 2 weeks before serving.

Toum is a Lebanese garlic sauce that is used in small amounts like butter to spread on a warm pita before rolling up with roasted chicken in the classic shawarma. Traditionally, toum is made with raw garlic that is whipped with lemon and oil to form a creamy, very potent white sauce similar to aioli. My recipe poaches the garlic in milk first to sweeten the garlic flavor. When you have this on hand, you can add a spoonful to dark leafy greens or sautéed vegetables, stir into soups, or simply as a sauce for roasted meats. ◆ **ANA**

MAKES 1 CUP

TOUM

¼ cup peeled garlic cloves

1½ cups whole milk

½ teaspoon kosher salt, plus more to taste

½ cup extra-virgin olive oil

1 tablespoon freshly squeezed lemon juice

Freshly ground black pepper

Combine the garlic and milk in a nonreactive or stainless steel 2-quart saucepan. Bring to a boil over high heat. Lower the heat to a simmer and cook until the garlic is soft when squeezed with a pair of tongs and the milk has thickened, about 25 minutes. Set aside to cool.

Combine the garlic, milk, salt, olive oil, and lemon juice in a blender and blend until very smooth and creamy. Season with salt and pepper to taste. Use immediately or cover and refrigerate in an airtight container for up to 5 days.

The French call this *beurre noisette* (hazelnut butter) because the butter smells like hazelnuts when it caramelizes. The result is a concentrated, sweet, nutty butter flavor. You can use less brown butter in a recipe than you would regular butter and expect to get the same, if not slightly more, flavor. I like to brown a pound of butter at a time so that I have it on hand to use instead of butter for sautéing sugar snap peas, scrambling eggs, coating pasta, or making Tomato–Brown Butter (page 214). It's also wonderful served at room temperature and spread on bread or toast. ◆ **ANA**

MAKES 12 OUNCES OR 1½ CUPS

BROWN BUTTER

4 sticks (1 pound)
unsalted butter

Have a dry fine-mesh sieve and stainless steel bowl ready before you start making the brown butter. If there is any water, the butter will bubble vigorously and can be dangerous, so please make sure that your bowl, ladle, and sieve are not wet.

Bring the butter to a boil in a heavy 2-quart saucepan over medium heat, then lower the heat to medium-low or low. Simmer until it turns brown and smells like hazelnuts, about 10 minutes.

The butter will clarify first. The solids will sink to the bottom after the water has evaporated. It can burn quickly (turning from brown to black), so you must watch it carefully after 6 minutes of simmering. As soon as you smell a toasted nut aroma, check the butter by ladling a little bit onto a white plate. If it looks like maple syrup, it is done. Strain the brown butter immediately through the sieve into the bowl and allow it to cool. Cover and refrigerate for up to 1 month, or freeze for up to 3 months.

I first tasted this sauce in Turkey on the famous Iskender kebab. Iskender is composed of lightly toasted bread (thicker than pita but thinner than focaccia) that was bathed in tomato sauce, basted with brown butter, and topped with cubes of grilled beef; charred long, thin green peppers; and plenty of yogurt. You will love this nutty, rich tomato sauce because caramelizing the butter intensifies the flavors and balances the acidity. I use this sauce in place of regular tomato sauce on many things, even pasta. It works hand-in-hand with yogurt and gets even better when you add a teaspoon each of dried mint, sumac, and Turkish red pepper flakes. ◆ **ANA**

MAKES 2½ CUPS

TOMATO–BROWN BUTTER

1 (14.5-ounce) can crushed tomatoes

2 cloves garlic, finely chopped

1 tablespoon extra-virgin olive oil

¼ cup brown butter (page 213)

Kosher salt and freshly ground black pepper

Combine the tomatoes, garlic, olive oil, and brown butter in a 10-inch sauté pan over low heat and simmer until the tomatoes start to break down and become soft and jamlike, about 20 minutes. Set aside to cool.

Blend until smooth, then season with salt and pepper to taste. Use warm or hot. Store, covered in the refrigerator, for up to 1 week.

Clarifying butter is the process of separating the milk solids and water from the butterfat. Using clarified butter, or just the butterfat, with phyllo dough gives the pastry crispier layers because the moisture has been removed. When the butterfat is separated out, you will lose about 25 percent of the volume of the butter. ◆ **MAURA**

MAKES 1½ CUPS

CLARIFIED BUTTER

4 sticks (1 pound) unsalted butter

Melt the butter in a saucepan over low heat. Skim off the foam with a spoon as it rises to the surface. Remove the pan from the heat and set aside to cool. Skim off any foam that rises. Pour into a small container and refrigerate. Because we have removed the milk solids, clarified butter keeps for up to 3 months in the refrigerator.

Zhoug is a spicy herb sauce of Yemenite origin that you find in Syria and Israel. It's often the go-to condiment for falafel and is eaten with bread for those who want heat with every bite. It's a must with Shakshuka (page 9), and you'll probably find yourself stirring it into scrambled eggs, spreading it on a sandwich, mixing it with Greek yogurt to make a dip, or just eating it by the spoonful. ◆ **ANA**

MAKES 1¼ CUPS

ZHOUG

2 Hungarian wax peppers, stemmed and coarsely chopped (seeds are good) (see Cook's Note, below)

1½ cups fresh cilantro leaves (from one large bunch or two small ones)

1½ cups fresh flat-leaf parsley leaves (from one bunch)

2 cloves peeled garlic

½ teaspoon kosher salt

1 teaspoon ground coriander

1 teaspoon ground cumin

½ cup extra-virgin olive oil

1½ teaspoons sherry vinegar

Combine all the ingredients in a blender and blend until very smooth. You should have a bright green emulsified sauce. Use immediately or cover and refrigerate in an airtight container for up to 5 days.

COOK'S NOTE We suggest using Hungarian wax peppers because they are medium-spicy and have a lot of flesh, which helps give the zhoug some body and texture. If you can't find these peppers, use jalapeños instead.

Also known as advieh, this aromatic blend comes from Persian cuisine. It's fragrant, a little sweet, and gently warming. It is delicious mixed with sugar and sprinkled over baked goods, donuts, and rice pudding or added to dried fruits that are cooking into jam. It straddles the sweet and savory world because it's also great for flavoring rice pilaf with toasted nuts, lentil soup, lamb meatballs, braised chicken, or vegetable stew. It's a blend that is shared by chefs and pastry chefs. ◆ **ANA**

MAKES ABOUT ⅓ CUP

PERSIAN SPICE

¼ cup dried organic rose petals (available online)

¼ cup ground cinnamon

1 tablespoon freshly ground black pepper

½ teaspoon ground cardamom

1 teaspoon ground nutmeg

1 teaspoon ground coriander

Pass the rose petals through a medium-mesh sieve into a small mixing bowl to remove any bits of stem and to grind them into a fine powder. Add the cinnamon, pepper, cardamom, nutmeg, and coriander and stir to blend. Store in an airtight container out of direct sunlight for up to 3 months.

This blend gives our Chicken Shawarma (page 103) its zest. The well-balanced combination of sweet spices like allspice and cinnamon with earthy black pepper is typical of Lebanese cooking. We often think of allspice and cinnamon during the holidays in mulled cider or pumpkin pie and, in general, associate them with something sweet—but in a blend like this, the flavors work well on big thick slices of heirloom tomato in the summer and on grilled or roasted chicken, beef, or lamb. Just a half teaspoon added to a few cups of tomato sauce can transform and add bold aromatics to a rice pilaf or vegetable gratin. If you designate a Krups-style coffee and spice grinder for spices, you can grind the peppercorns and spices like coriander seed and cumin seed yourself for fuller, fresher flavor. Just wipe the spice grinder clean with a paper towel after using. ◆ **ANA**

MAKES ABOUT ¾ CUP

SHAWARMA SPICE

¼ cup freshly ground
black pepper

2 tablespoons freshly ground
white pepper

¼ cup ground allspice

1 tablespoon ground cinnamon

1 tablespoon ground cumin

1 tablespoon ground nutmeg

1 tablespoon ground coriander

Combine all the spices in a small mixing bowl and stir to blend. Store in an airtight container out of direct sunlight for up to 3 months.

In Arabic, *baharat* has two meanings. It refers to this particular spice mix and it also means "flowers and seeds" or is more loosely translated to "herbs and spices." Many spice shops in the Middle East are simply called baharat. Baharat is packed with diverse aromas—some peppery, some sweet, some earthy—but no one flavor dominates. And there are as many different blends of baharat as there are people who make it. The mixture varies from family to family and from spice shop to spice shop, but conveys all the romantic fragrances and everything that spice is. Sofra's version of baharat is very versatile and is wonderful with grilled lamb, roasted chicken, all soups, squashes, pumpkin, and carrot salads. This blend is my number-one go-to and most frequently used spice blend at home. ◆ **ANA**

MAKES ½ CUP

BAHARAT SPICE

2 tablespoons dried oregano

2 tablespoons dried spearmint

1 tablespoon ground cinnamon

1 tablespoon ground nutmeg

1 tablespoon ground cumin

1 tablespoon ground coriander

2 tablespoons freshly ground black pepper

1½ teaspoons ground allspice

Pass the dried oregano and dried mint through a medium-mesh sieve into a small mixing bowl to remove any bits of stem and to grind them into a fine powder. Add the cinnamon, nutmeg, cumin, coriander, pepper, and allspice and stir to blend. Store in an airtight container out of direct sunlight for up to 3 months.

I discovered this recipe in a very old New England cookbook. At Oleana and Sofra, we are always looking for a twist, and pumpkin jam seemed like a great alternative to traditional pumpkin desserts. This jam has become a signature item. It is so versatile, you can use it instead of raspberries in turnovers (page 40), or add a layer of it to the cheese filling in the Kunefe (page 190). It is great with toast and cheese or simply added to your coffee. ◆ **MAURA**

MAKES 5½ CUPS

PUMPKIN JAM

1 (2-pound) roasting pumpkin

2 pounds sugar

1½ teaspoons ground cinnamon, plus more if needed

½ teaspoon ground nutmeg, plus more if needed

½ teaspoon ground cloves, plus more if needed

1 teaspoon kosher salt

To make the pumpkin puree, cut the pumpkin into 4- to 5-inch pieces. Remove the fiber and seeds with a spoon. Put the pieces in a steamer basket. Place in a pot of boiling water. Cover with foil and pierce a few holes in the foil with a knife. Steam until smooth and very soft, about 40 minutes. Keep an eye on the amount of water in the pot and refill as needed. Set aside to cool.

Spoon out the flesh and puree in a food processor.

Combine the cooked pumpkin and sugar in a large pot. Cook over medium heat, stirring well until the sugar dissolves and liquefies, 5 minutes. Lower the heat and cook until the mixture thickens and turns a darker orange color, about 20 minutes.

Add the cinnamon, nutmeg, and cloves. Adjust spices to taste.

The jam will keep in the refrigerator for 2 months.

Fragrant and beautiful pink roses arrive from the beaches of Westport, Massachusetts, every June thanks to Eva Sommaripa, a local farmer. We usually get them all at once, so we have a few days of spreading love and smiles around the kitchen as this jam boils away. You can use any rose petals that are not sprayed, but the wild beach roses (*Rosa rugosa*) are our favorite. This jam is a great addition to ice cream, yogurt, and to our Almond Rose Cake (page 185), Persian Love Cake (page 183), Milk Pie (page 175), and Kunefe (page 190). ◆ **MAURA**

MAKES 1 CUP

ROSE PETAL JAM

2 cups sugar

2 cups water

3 cups lightly packed pink beach rose petals

1 tablespoon freshly squeezed lemon juice

2 teaspoons rose water

Combine the sugar and water in a large saucepan and bring to a boil, stirring until the sugar dissolves, about 1 minute. Add the rose petals, pressing them into the syrup with a spoon. Lower the heat to medium and cook at a low boil until reduced by one-third, 20 to 25 minutes. To check for doneness, spoon some syrup onto a cold plate. If you can run the spoon through the syrup and the line remains, remove from the heat.

Add the lemon juice and rose water and set aside to cool to room temperature. The jam will set up as it chills. The jam will keep in the refrigerator for up to 6 months.

This combination is commonly found in a classic Moroccan pie called bisteeya, usually made with chicken or pigeon, pairing the meat with cinnamon and sugar for a savory dish. We use these in our Olive Oil Granola (page 37). I love these on yogurt, the savory background of the olive oil creates a perfect balance with the creamy tart flavor. Also delicious on ice cream, our Milk Pie (page 175), or try them with your chicken. ◆ **MAURA**

MAKES 2 CUPS

MOROCCAN SPICED ALMONDS

2 cups sliced natural (skin-on) raw almonds

1 tablespoon extra-virgin olive oil

¼ cup Demerara sugar or other raw sugar

½ teaspoon fleur de sel or kosher salt

1½ teaspoons ground cinnamon

Preheat the oven to 350°F. Line a rimmed baking sheet with parchment paper.

Toss the almonds and olive oil in a large bowl, coating the almonds well. Spread on the prepared baking sheet and bake until lightly toasted, about 10 minutes. Remove the almonds from the oven and let cool for 15 minutes; they should still be a little warm.

Combine the sugar, salt, and cinnamon in a bowl. Add the almonds and toss with a rubber spatula to coat completely. The sugar will stick better if the almonds are slightly warm but not hot enough to melt the sugar.

Spread out on the baking sheet until to cool completely. Store in an airtight container for up to 1 month.

These boldly spiced sliced almonds are used in a couple of different recipes in this book. I love to snack on them. The spice and saltiness is addictive but they also make a great accompaniment to a cheese plate. ◆ **MAURA**

MAKES 2 CUPS

ZA'ATAR SPICED ALMONDS

2 cups sliced natural (skin-on) raw almonds

2 tablespoons extra-virgin olive oil

½ cup za'atar (see page 245)

1 tablespoon sumac

Grated zest of 2 lemons

2 teaspoons fleur de sel or kosher salt

1 tablespoon toasted sesame seeds (see page 241)

Preheat the oven to 350°F. Line a rimmed baking sheet with parchment paper.

Toss the almonds and olive oil in large bowl, coating the almonds well. Spread on the prepared baking sheet and bake until lightly toasted, about 10 minutes. Remove the almonds from the oven and let cool for 15 minutes; they should still be a little warm.

Combine the za'atar, sumac, lemon zest, salt, and sesame seeds in a bowl. Add the almonds and toss with a rubber spatula to coat completely.

Spread out on the baking sheet to cool completely. Store in an airtight container for up to 2 weeks.

ESSENTIAL INGREDIENTS

Some ingredients are essential for achieving authentic Middle Eastern flavors, and it is worth seeking out a marketplace or specialty shop that you trust so that you can have them on hand to prepare the recipes in this book. We hope you will find many uses for them, and that they become ingredients you can't live without. We have all of our essential pantry ingredients available at Sofra, so that we can share them with our customers.

ALMOND FLOUR

Made from finely ground almonds, almond flour (sometimes called almond meal) is what remains after the nuts are ground and the oils are pressed out of the nuts. You can use almond flour made from blanched or natural almonds for Sesame Financiers (page 196) and Persian Love Cake (page 183). It is available at Trader Joe's, many specialty food stores, and from Bob's Red Mill (bobsredmill.com).

ALMOND PASTE

Made from ground almonds and sugar in equal parts, almond paste is widely available at supermarkets or specialty food stores. It comes in tubes or cans. You can also find it at americanalmond.com in the Love 'n Bake line.

BULGUR WHEAT

Our favorite whole grain for cooking and eating is bulgur. This partially cooked, dried, cracked wheat is available in varying grades, from fine (#1) to coarse (#4). The #1 fine is not milled as much as flour but can be used similarly to thicken a liquid or to make kibbeh by reconstituting the grain in hot water and kneading it to make a dough. The #4 coarse is delicious cooked like rice to make a rich, nutty pilaf.

CACAO NIBS

We are big fans of cacao nibs. They are the actual cacao bean that has been roasted and broken into tiny pieces. They add a slightly nutty and bitter flavor and are a way to add chocolate taste without using chocolate. Available from tazachocolate.com.

DATE MOLASSES

We use date molasses or date syrup (also called date honey and silan) interchangeably. Both are made by boiling dates and reducing them to a sweet, fruity syrup. Date syrup is more versatile than the traditional date molasses, which is darker and more bitter. You can use it as an alternative sweetener on yogurt or ice cream or in coffee. Date syrup is available from ilovedatelady.com or amazon.com.

DATES

There are many different date varieties. Medjool dates are grown in California and are considered one of the best varieties, especially for baking. They are full and soft with a hint of caramel and honey flavor. They are widely available in supermarkets.

DEMERARA SUGAR

This is a large-grain, coarse, raw sugar similar to brown sugar with a light caramel flavor. It is usually partially refined, so it holds moisture better than regular brown sugar. Unlike brown sugar, it does not have added molasses.

DRIED MINT AND OREGANO

These are two out of three dried herbs we use most often. They marry nicely and can be used interchangeably. Each offers a very distinct Eastern Mediterranean taste.

The flavor of dried mint is likely most familiar to you in tea form. However, its sweet, warm notes are perfect for cooking. Use dried mint in place of oregano in a tomato sauce for sweeter flavors or add a spoonful to a cucumber-yogurt sauce, and you'll be hooked. In Turkey, dried mint means dried spearmint. This is the variety that is cooked with most often. Other mints, like peppermint, are great for teas or sweet pastry preparations but don't have the same warmth or subtle sweetness.

Turkish and Greek oregano offer warm, earthy flavors. There are several different species that grow wild and are foraged all over Greece, where the herb is known as rigani. Our contractor, Max Hatziiliades, supplies us with rigani harvested by his family on Mount Olympus. It's difficult to find oregano of the same quality outside of Greece, but look for Turkish or Greek species. You can find the Turkish variety at penzeys.com, and any Greek grocer or specialty shop should carry some rigani.

FETA CHEESE

If you are Greek, there is no messing around with feta; feta comes from Greece and Greece only. That being said, I love using sheep's milk feta for certain recipes like whipped feta or melted feta because it's creamy from higher butterfat. For salads, I prefer the barrel-aged feta from Greece that crumbles nicely. Feta is always brined and cured but can be found made with different milks—sheep, cow, and goat.

GRAPE MOLASSES

Grape molasses, or pekmez, as it is known in Turkey, is commonly found in Turkish homes and used the way we use granulated sugar. It is produced in Anatolia by reducing grapes to a syrup after hours of boiling. One of the most popular breakfast items in Turkey is a combination of tahini and pekmez. It is also rich in calcium and potassium, so some parents feed a spoonful to their children every day. Store it in its jar at room temperature.

GREEK YOGURT AND LABNE

Yogurt is an essential part of cooking anything and everything Middle Eastern. It adds acidity, sourness, fat, and creamy texture to a dish. Yogurt is the heavy cream of the Middle East, but with more dimension and less fat. Here in the States, there is a whole

To make your own labne, line a colander with cheesecloth and place a mixing bowl underneath it to catch the liquid that drains from the yogurt. Put 4 cups plain whole-milk Greek yogurt (the ingredients should include only milk and cultures and no thickeners) in the colander and wrap the cheesecloth over the top. Place a small saucer or plate on top to lightly press it down. Refrigerate at least overnight, or for up to 2 days. Store covered in the refrigerator for up to 10 days.

grocery store aisle dedicated to yogurt that wasn't there five to six years ago. Shopping for yogurt is confusing, and most "Greek" yogurts on the shelf aren't Greek. Real Greek yogurt and labne don't have thickeners like carrageenan in them. They're made with whole milk and strained to remove water, making them thick.

Find a whole-milk Greek yogurt or labne with as few ingredients as possible and you'll be happy. Unless you make it yourself, you'll battle with the labels, so pick one that you think tastes good (like Fage) and be sure not to skimp on the fat. If you have to avoid dairy fat, add a little bit of olive oil to the recipe for a creamier mouthfeel.

HALOUMI CHEESE

Haloumi cheese is a sheep's milk cheese from Cyprus that is cooked and then brined. Because it is cooked, it can be sliced and put straight in a pan to caramelize without being breaded. It's best eaten very hot; it has a squeaky texture like cheese curds when it cools down. Haloumi is often seasoned with dried spearmint, which adds a sweet warmth to the cheese.

HALVAH

The word *halvah* can be used to refer to sweets or desserts, but it is mainly used to mean tahini halvah, a flaky, dense sesame candy that is one of the most popular desserts in the Middle East. It is sold in blocks in Middle Eastern specialty stores.

HARISSA

Great to have on hand, this well-known Tunisian condiment is used to perk up almost anything. It's the Mediterranean's answer to sriracha and has flavors like cumin, coriander, and caraway, and sometimes even rose. Harissa is medium-hot but rich with spices. Store it in the refrigerator to finish sauces, soups, or sandwiches. We love the brand Harissa Entube, which is available on Amazon.

HONEY

We love experimenting with different flavors of honey. You can really alter the flavor of a dish by using a bold-flavored honey. You can brush the Sesame Financiers (page 196) with a chestnut

honey, buckwheat honey, or pine honey if you can find it. Go with something more floral on the Persian Love Cake (page 183); our favorites are linden flower honey and sunflower honey. In the Sesame Cashew Bars (page 159), we use a raw honey from Champlain Valley Apiaries in Vermont, because we prefer something thick to create the caramel layer. Don't be afraid to experiment or splurge on a special jar of honey, or start a honey collection of your own.

KASSERI CHEESE

This is a Greek or Turkish table cheese typically made with sheep's milk. It has a semihard consistency that is great for grating and melting with a sweet, nutty flavor more mild than that of gruyère. Gruyère is a fine substitute if kasseri can't be found. I find it at Whole Foods or the Greek and Armenian stores in the Boston area.

KATAIFI PASTRY

Often described as shredded phyllo, kataifi is made from a batter that is poured through a funnel sieve onto a spinning griddle over very high heat. It cooks instantly and is removed from the hot plate like a lock of long golden hair with a crisp, shredded-wheat texture. This pastry is more fun and easier to work with than phyllo, and you'll end up wrapping lots of things, like nut fillings, with it. It's normally sold frozen or in the refrigerated section of the store in boxes. Take what you need from the box and keep it in a zip-top bag while you wait for it to defrost (usually it can be used within 10 minutes of being pulled from the freezer) and wrap the rest tightly back up to keep frozen up to 1 month. Pull strands from the "rope" of pastry in the box if you need to measure it, and pack it into the measuring cup or pull strands about ¼ inch thick to make small ropes to coil around fillings.

MARAS PEPPER OR ALEPPO PEPPER

True Aleppo pepper hasn't been available in America since the crisis in Syria began. In southeastern Turkey, not far from the border with Syria and around the city of Kahramanmaras, is the Maras region, where these sweet oily peppers thrive and are usually what is imported and labeled as Aleppo pepper. You will find a shaker of Maras red pepper flakes on the table in every kebab joint in Turkey. Bright red, brightly flavored, and oily, with a bittersweet, slow, mild heat, these peppers broaden all the other flavors in a dish.

You can replace those red pepper flakes that you have in the cabinet (the ones that you see in a shaker in a pizzeria) with Maras pepper. It will change your life and your recipes for the better. If you don't go through it as fast as we do, keep some on hand in the freezer. Our friends and neighbors at formaggiokitchen.com (located in Cambridge) have beautiful Maras pepper.

MASTIC

Used sparingly, mastic adds a beautiful, slightly pinelike flavor to desserts. It is the resin obtained from the mastic tree on the Greek island of Chios. Once it is taken from the tree, it is sun-dried into tiny translucent pieces. It is sold in small quantities because a little is all you need. It is best to grind it with a mortar and pestle with just a tiny pinch of sugar. Using the sugar will prevent you from grinding it into a paste or gum. Mastic can be found at Middle Eastern specialty stores. Store sealed at room temperature.

NIGELLA SEEDS

Nigella look a lot like black sesame seeds, but they are not related. The shape is a little more edgy or rigid and the flavor is savory and slightly nutty, with a hint of onion or celery. They flavor a lot of savory flatbreads and crackers in the Middle East and are often used to flavor string cheese. Store in an airtight jar out of the light like other spices.

NUTS

Toasting nuts is an important detail. If you compare a toasted nut to a natural one, you will instantly notice the texture and flavor is enhanced by toasting. If the recipe requires toasted nuts, it is best to chop them before toasting them; by doing that, you can use them sooner and you can discard any of the dust or particles

of nuts that are too small. Already ground walnuts are readily available in supermarkets. We prefer to use these in the Milky Walnut-Fig Baklava (page 170), Marzipan Cookies with Figs and Walnuts (page 155) and Cheese and Honey Fatayer (page 138) because the smaller nuts distribute more evenly.

Natural sliced almonds are used in the Moroccan Spiced Almonds (page 227) and the Za'atar Spiced Almonds (page 229). These are almonds with the skin still on them. Store nuts in a covered container in your refrigerator for best results.

OLIVE OIL

Olive oil is the most essential ingredient in Mediterranean cuisine because it brings fat, sweet vegetal flavors and silky textures to a dish. Unless we are searing meat at extremely high temperatures or deep-frying, we never use any type of oil other than extra-virgin olive oil. It breaks down at high temperatures but when you sweat vegetables, sauté, or simmer a sauce, its sweet fruit flavor infuses the dish.

We cook with two varietals of olive oil. Olympiana Early Harvest from Extra Virgin Foods is made from koroneiki olives on an estate just outside of Kalamata, Greece. It has a bold, grassy, and fruity flavor with very low acidity that is perfect for salads and vegetable meze. Our friend Paul Hatziiliades is the founder of Olympiana, and his father, Max, built all three of our restaurants, including Sofra. Paul has an incredible palate for delicious oil and is a stickler for quality. Learn more at extravirginfoods.com.

Our friend Chafic Malouf presses the other oil we adore. We visited his Sourani olive orchard in Koura, Lebanon, in the late fall of 2011. We fell in love with his buttery, sweet, and grassy oil. His oil is milder than most Greek oils and its versatility makes it work with everything. Chafic's oil is available at many locations in Massachusetts or at oliveharvest.com.

Recently, we've discovered California Arbequina oil from California Olive Ranch, a high-quality domestic brand with a smooth flavor and hints of green apple. It is available at Whole Foods and online at californiaoliveranch.com.

Store olive oil in a cool, dark place. Heat and light will make it break down and go rancid.

ORANGE BLOSSOM WATER

Our favorite orange blossom water is Mymouné brand. We fell in love with it on our trip to Lebanon. It is made by distilling bitter orange blossoms. Orange blossom water is a beautiful addition to caramel and goes great with chocolate, making it an essential item in a pastry. We have found that some Lebanese recipes combine rose water and orange blossom water in the same item. When you use something as subtle and balanced as Mymouné, you can take the chance. Store at room temperature.

PERSIAN CUCUMBERS

These small cucumbers, sometimes labeled "baby cucumbers," are now common in grocery stores all over. The skin is thin, the seeds are small and few, the water content is low, and the fragrance is astonishing. They are worth using in any recipe or snack that calls for a cucumber. We suggest you make the switch; you'll be glad. Persian cucumbers are half the size of an English cucumber, which usually comes individually wrapped. English cukes are my second choice for similar characteristics but have larger seeds, more water, and thicker skin that may need to be peeled if tough.

POMEGRANATE MOLASSES

Pomegranate molasses is not actually molasses but rather a syrup made from the juice of sour pomegranates cooked down with a little salt and sometimes sugar. It's tart, sweet, and acidic and can be used in place of vinegar or lemon. Making it is very labor intensive, but it preserves the abundant pomegranate crops throughout the Middle East. Unfortunately, there are many commercial brands that add too much sugar and coloring to offset the cost of labor and fruit.

This pantry gem brightens a rich stew after it has been braised all day and adds intensity and acidity to meze dishes. It makes a wonderful dressing for fattoush (page 73) and a great glaze for roasted lamb or chicken. Store in a cool, dark pantry once it's opened. My favorite brand, Mymouné, is made by a cooperative at the foot of Mount Sannine in Lebanon. It is available at some Middle Eastern specialty stores, sofrabakery.com, or mymoune.com.

ROSE WATER

Known as *ma-ward* in Arabic, rose water is made by distilling red and pink roses. The Turkish people cherish roses; the beauty and aroma of these flowers are truly valued. In Lebanon, the subtle use of rose water is simply beautiful. Use a very light touch, just a capful or half capful, when experimenting with new recipes. It is available online and in more and more Middle Eastern stores. Our preferred rose water is Mymouné brand from Lebanon. Store at room temperature.

SALT

All of our recipes are made with kosher salt, which has much more flavor than iodized table salt. When sifting dry ingredients, sift first, then add the kosher salt; it should not go through the sifter. Some recipes call for fleur de sel, a variety of sea salt from the Brittany region of France. Its coarseness adds texture to the Moroccan Spiced Almonds (page 227) and Za'atar Spiced Almonds (page 229), where it will be noticed. It is also good for finishing salads, vegetables, and chocolate.

SEMOLINA FLOUR

Semolina is made from coarsely grinding the heart of durum wheat kernels, which is the hard part of the grain that is left after milling the flour. We use it as a thickener to make milk puddings and custards and as flour in our Revani (page 193). Store in an airtight container at room temperature.

SESAME SEEDS

Sesame seeds may be the oldest condiment known to man. They have a high oil content and are the main ingredient in tahini. You can buy them toasted or untoasted. We prefer to buy them toasted for baking purposes because they are drier and will stick to what you are baking more easily. To toast your own sesame seeds, use a small nonstick pan over medium-low heat and spread sesame seeds in an even layer in the pan. Stir them every 30 seconds and continue to toast them until they are golden brown, about 4 minutes.

SUJUK

Sujuk is a lamb and/or beef sausage that has been cured with spices like fenugreek, cumin, chiles, and garlic. The chiles in the sausage turn the cooking fat red, which is delicious for flavoring—and coloring—eggs, rice, bean dishes, and bread. Most sujuk is dry cured.

SUMAC

Sumac is a spice that is derived from the berries of a tree that grows throughout the Mediterranean and the Middle East. The closest relative in the United States in flavor is the common staghorn sumac, which grows wild like a weed. The fruit itself consists of clusters of purplish red berries. When dried or cured with salt, it tastes sour, raisiny, and lemony. When a dish requires astringency, use this in place of lemon or vinegar to get similar but richer results. The shelf life of good sumac is less than a year. Use the spice with a heavy hand or by the teaspoon sprinkled over salad, chicken, or fish. You can find sumac in most Middle Eastern grocery stores or online.

TAHINI

This paste is made with hulled sesame seeds. It has a bittersweet, nutty flavor and a wonderful creamy texture. Tahini is an essential ingredient in many signature Middle Eastern dishes, among them hummus and baba ganoush. Some commercial tahinis are very bitter, often rancid, and have a chalky texture. If the tahini seems bitter, try adding some salt, which will help pull some of the bitterness out. As the sesame paste sits, the oil separates, so the mixture should be stirred before it's used. We recommend storing it in the refrigerator after it's opened.

We love the brand Tohum, which is a dark-roasted organic tahini from Turkey (tohum.com). It is available at specialty grocers or on Amazon. We also recommend the super-fresh tahini from Brooklyn Sesame, which you can order at brooklynsesame.com, and the ultracreamy Soom brand (soomfoods.com) from Philadelphia, which you can find online from several sources.

TOMATO PASTE

To make tomato paste, ripe tomatoes are cooked until the tomatoes burst apart. The skins and seeds are strained out and the juice is evaporated into a thick paste. Using a spoonful will add umami and body to almost any dish or sauce. We love combining tomato paste and red pepper paste in equal amounts when seasoning red lentils, soups, and marinades or trying to pack a vinaigrette with flavor. The best quality is always found when the ingredients are simple, so be sure to read labels. I prefer the Tukas brand, which can be found in many Middle Eastern markets and online at www.tulumba.com. The paste can be divided up into small containers and frozen.

TURKISH RED PEPPER PASTE

Red pepper paste is a concentration of cooked, lightly salted, sweet and hot peppers traditionally dried in the sun. It's made the same way that tomato paste is made and is used similarly for depth. Packed with umami and sweet, spicy vegetal flavors, a teaspoon can add a lot of body and structure to a vegetable-based dish. It also makes a great rub for lamb when mixed with Baharat Spice (page 221) and olive oil. In the markets in towns like Gaziantep in the southeast of Turkey, one can enjoy these pepper pastes in a variety of heats and concentrations by the spoonful. It is hard to come by the same quality in the United States. We rely on the Turkish brand Tukas. You may want to empty a large jar of paste into four smaller containers and freeze three of them. There are many brands available at tulumba.com.

URFA PEPPER

Urfa is named after the city Sanliurfa in southeastern Turkey near the Syrian border. It is a deep blackish red chile, with an earthy, raisiny flavor that is slightly bitter, like coffee or chocolate. It is often briefly fermented after drying, which lends a dark color and deep umami flavor. Normally, Urfa pepper is sold coarsely ground so that you can sprinkle it over anything. It pairs well with grilled meats, eggplant, chocolate, and tomatoes. You can shop for the real deal online at formaggiokitchen.com.

ZA'ATAR

Za'atar is the third dried herb we use most often, after mint and oregano. The word *za'atar* refers to the wild herb itself and also to a blend of the wild herb with sumac and sesame seeds. There are many species of za'atar that grow throughout the Eastern Mediterranean, from different regions, countries, villages, and so on. Za'atar is related to thyme and is often used interchangeably with thyme to keep it simple, but it is very different from the species that is common in the U.S. The flavor of the herb za'atar is very similar to that of summer savory. When the herb is dried and blended with sumac and sesame seeds, you can mix it with olive oil to form a paste and spread that paste on anything. You'll crave its flavor and find yourself putting it on warm olives, yogurt, feta cheese, roasted chicken, flatbreads, and even cheese pizza, to perk it up. Eat it by the spoonful. You can shop for an excellent blend at mymoune.com or splurge and get the best-quality blend from our friend and master spice blender Lior at La Boîte (laboiteny.com).

FRIENDS AND RESOURCES

Brooklynsesame.com
Tahini

Californiaoliveranch.com
Olive oil

Champlainvalleyhoney.com
Honey

Extravirginfoods.com
Olive oil, cheeses

Formaggiokitchen.com
Spices, charcuterie, cheeses,
condiments

Ilovedatelady.com
Dates

Laboiteny.com
Spices

Mymoune.com
Flower waters, jams,
pomegranate molasses

Oliveharvest.com
Olive oil

Penzeys.com
Spices

Soomfoods.com
Tahini

Tazachocolate.com
Chocolate

Tohum.com
Tahini

Tulumba.com
Maras red pepper

ABOUT THE AUTHORS

ANA SORTUN

Cited as one of the country's "best creative fusion practitioners," Seattle-born Ana Sortun graduated from La Varenne Ecole de Cuisine de Paris before opening Moncef Medeb's Aigo Bistro in Concord, Massachusetts, in the early 1990s. Following stints at 8 Holyoke and Casablanca in Harvard Square, she opened Oleana in 2001, immediately drawing raves for dishes that the *New York Times* described as "rustic-traditional and deeply inventive." Corby Kummer has hailed Ana's "culinary genius" in both *Boston* magazine and *Saveur*. Awarded the Best Chef: Northeast honor by the James Beard Foundation in 2005, her cookbook *Spice* was published in 2006 and has become a bestseller.

Ana and business partner executive pastry chef Maura Kilpatrick opened Sofra Bakery & Café in Cambridge (2008), which offers a unique style of foods and baked goods influenced mostly by the countries of Turkey, Lebanon, and Greece. Ana has also opened Sarma, a traditional Turkish-style tavern featuring meze.

When she is not at one of the restaurants, you might find Ana on a culinary tour of Turkey with the Oldways Preservation Trust, which provide tours and educational programs focused on good health and eating.

MAURA KILPATRICK

After receiving a graduate certificate in baking at the California Culinary Academy, Maura moved back to her hometown of Boston and worked for many of the city's top chefs including Lydia Shire, Moncef Medeb, Rene Michelena, and Ana Sortun. She opened two bakeries shortly thereafter with High-Rise Bread Company. In 2001, she reunited with Ana to develop the concept for Oleana. It was at that time that Maura fell in love with the exotic flavors and spices for which she is now known. Through extensive research, experimentation, travel and "homework," Maura has perfected her award-winning Middle-Eastern pastries; integrating typical ingredients from the Eastern Mediterranean such as orange blossoms, tahini, and rose petals. She creates contemporary versions of traditional desserts from Turkey, Egypt, and beyond.

Maura has been recognized with flawless reviews by local press and magazines and has distinguished herself as an executive pastry chef and bakery owner. She was voted Best Pastry Chef by *Boston* magazine readers in 2002, 2007, 2008, 2009 and 2011. Sofra Bakery was also awarded the distinction of Best Bakery in 2009 and Best Breakfast in 2015, also by *Boston* Magazine.

Most recently, Maura was a nominee for the 2015 and 2016 James Beard Award for Best Pastry Chef.

ACKNOWLEDGMENTS

This book would not have been possible without many other people. We are deeply grateful for their encouragement, commitment, and support.

We'd like to thank our entire staff at Sofra for the amazing work that they produce every single day. They make the guest experience at Sofra as delicious and special as possible.

We thank Lindsey Barcebal and James Moore for their testing and tasting skills! Many of our chefs and sous chefs, from Oleana, Sofra, and Sarma, were incredibly supportive and inspirational to us during the process of making this book.

Thanks to Gary Griffin, our business partner extraordinaire, for trusting us and tolerating all the hard work, time, and attention this took away from running our business.

Thanks to our agent, Lisa Ekus, who was a cheerleader, and of course to our editor, Kelly Snowden, and our art director, Betsy Stromberg, for the amazing guidance, patience, and magical bookmaking skills. Such a strong and creative team at Ten Speed!

Thank you to our writer, Sally Sampson, for coaxing out our ideas and then transforming them into clear words on the page.

Thank you Kristin Teig, our very talented photographer, who believed in this project deeply and along with food stylist master, Catrine Kelty, made such artful pictures. They made it effortless and natural.

Thank you to Ana's husband, Chris Kurth (and all the beautiful vegetables and ingredients that he provides us with), and Ana's daughter, Siena Kurth, for being so supportive as she needed extra time to write and edit.

To Maura's family, thank you for some of the wonderful recipes in these pages, and thank you for always being supportive and enthusiastic fans of Sofra. This book is a gift to all of you, especially Maura's mom and dad, who would be so happy to see this. We miss you every day.

We'd like to thank all our friends who believed in this book and believed in the success of Sofra, especially Max Hatziiliades, Richard Kzarian, Vartan Nalbandian, Joanne Reeves, and the team at Toth+Co.

And lastly, we'd like to thank all of our customers who have, over the years, continued to request this book and motivate us to write it.

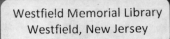

INDEX

Copyright © 2016 by Ana Sortun and Maura Kilpatrick
Photographs copyright © 2016 by Kristin Teig

All rights reserved.
Published in the United States by Ten Speed Press, an imprint
of the Crown Publishing Group, a division of Penguin Random
House LLC, New York.
www.crownpublishing.com
www.tenspeed.com

Ten Speed Press and the Ten Speed Press colophon are
registered trademarks of Penguin Random House LLC.

Library of Congress Cataloging-in-Publication Data
is on file with the publisher.

Hardcover ISBN: 978-1-60774-918-9
eBook ISBN: 978-1-60774-919-6

Printed in China

Design by Betsy Stromberg

10 9 8 7 6 5 4 3 2 1

First Edition